Chris Fullerton

Enter Mourning

For Avis.
with all my good
wishes

Enter Mourning

A MEMOIR ON DEATH, DEMENTIA, & COMING HOME

HEATHER MENZIES

KEY PORTER BOOKS

Library and Archives Canada Cataloguing in Publication

Menzies, Heather, 1949-
    Enter mourning : a memoir on death, dementia and
coming home / Heather Menzies.

ISBN 978-1-55470-155-1

    1. Menzies, Heather, 1949-. 2. Menzies, Heather, 1949- —Family.
3. Alzheimer's disease—Patients—Family relationships. 4. Alzheimer's
disease—Patients—Care. 5. Sandwich generation. 6. Mothers and
daughters. 7. Authors, Canadian (English)—20th century—Biography.
I. Title.

RC523.M46 2009   362.196'8310092   C2008-906780-0

ONTARIO ARTS COUNCIL
CONSEIL DES ARTS DE L'ONTARIO

The publisher gratefully acknowledges the support of the Canada Council for the Arts and the Ontario Arts Council for its publishing program. We acknowledge the support of the Government of Ontario through the Ontario Media Development Corporation's Ontario Book Initiative.

We acknowledge the financial support of the Government of Canada through the Book Publishing Industry Development Program (BPIDP) for our publishing activities.

Key Porter Books Limited
Six Adelaide Street East, Tenth Floor
Toronto, Ontario
Canada M5C 1H6

www.keyporter.com

Text design: Marijke Friesen
Electronic formatting: Alison Carr

Photo on page 2 by Janet Menzies. All other photos by Heather Menzies.

Printed and bound in Canada

09 10 11 12 13 5 4 3 2 1

To Mum and to each of us, the children she bore, raised and loved: Douglas, Janet, Heather, and Dick. With love.

Contents

Preface

"She's gone."

I looked at Norma standing in the doorway of her home. I'd just returned from a walk by the river, in the misty dusk of a rainy fall day. I had stopped by here to pick up my sister-in-law on my way back to the hospital, to continue the deathwatch as planned. Now I stared at her, the words 'she's gone' rattling around in my brain, incommunicado.

"Your brother just called from the hospital. Your mother's..."

I still can't remember what word she used next.

I had been primed. I had been prepared for her to be ... gone. The palliative-care nurse had taken me delicately and firmly aside when I arrived in the morning. "Your mother is dying," she said. "It wouldn't surprise me if she were gone within twelve hours."

Over the past three years, I had struggled to understand, to accept, and to be there for Mum as dementia stripped her of her ability to remember, to navigate her car, to dress herself, and, finally, to speak in whole sentences. I'd learned a new, old language vested in gestures and touch, enunciated through rhythm, tone and cadence. I'd discovered the lovely landscape of sitting side by side with Mum on her single residence bed, just holding hands. When a stroke and a broken hip took her down further, we became so attuned to each other it was as though the umbilical cord that had connected us at the beginning of my life had grown back between us at the end of hers. Then this morning, what might have been another stroke during the night had left her unable to surface, to wake up. She was in a coma.

I'd spent the day with Mum surrounded by the slight paraphernalia required at this stage for someone who can no longer move, no longer swallow, whose organs are shutting down, whose extremities are growing cold because the blood is hardly flowing anymore. There were tiny pink sponges on sticks to moisten the inside of her dehydrated mouth, Vaseline for her drying lips, lotions to comfort her hands, socks to warm her chilling feet. I had made good use of these, tending to Mum as she lay there breathing quietly, sometimes seeming to sigh. I was ready. No, I wasn't.

Oh, but Mum would have been pleased at how well I handled it all. Norma offered to drive, but I was okay. We even talked along the way. Normal talk though I can't remember what about. I was calm, focused on the traffic, dwindling now with the ebbing of the rush hour. I negotiated the turn into the hospital grounds, drove to the visitors' parking lot, got a ticket, found a spot, turned off the engine, and got out.

It had stopped raining completely by now, and the air hung still around us. Norma and I walked toward the hospital, and I could see what I guessed to be the window of the room where Mum had spent the day and I with her except for the necessary phone calls to my sister Janet in Arizona and my brother Dick in Montreal, and to give Doug, the oldest, some time alone with Mum when he came at lunch time, and after work. Looking up, I remember being glad to see that the light in her room was still on.

Suddenly it was as though a wind had got up. I felt a tumbling rush of something coming toward me, something churning in the air. It was like a whirlwind of fall leaves that sometimes blow up from the sidewalk, only soft, like feathers. The sound, the feel was gentle against my face, yet fierce with energy.

"She's here," I said, my voice cracking from within this whirling, enveloping sensation.

Norma's arm came up around my shoulder.

"Of course," she said, as though this was the most natural thing in the world. She kept her arm there, guiding me as I stumbled forward, crying and trying to talk at the same time.

"She's come to meet us," I said, aware of some part of me stepping outside, saying "us" though suspecting that Norma had experienced nothing.

Inside, we took the elevator to the third floor, turned right into the main hall, walked down its neon-white strip of cluttered busyness then left into the Geriatric wing.

It came again: the sensation of air rushing toward me. The tears flowed. "She's saying it's okay," I said. I can't remember having taken this in as words spoken, more as meaning implanted firmly as a kiss. She wanted to comfort me, to say a last goodbye. I knew this absolutely.

I walked into the room where my brother Doug sat stoically beside our mother's frail, shrivelled, and utterly still body. She looked exactly as I'd left her two hours previously, having used a sponge-stick to moisten her lips and refresh the inside of her mouth, brushed her hair as her head lay on the pillow, and tucked her red velour dressing gown close around her, against the encroaching cold.

Nothing much had changed except that she'd stopped breathing. She'd slipped away. The journey we'd been on for the last few years and, intensively, for the last four weeks, was complete—for her, at least.

Introduction

At some point, taking care of my aging mother stopped being an imposition, or even a series of tasks I managed with some semblance of grace, and became an experience that changed my life. It opened me up to not just the unknown but to unknowing as a way of living, simultaneously letting go and letting in. I learned to give myself over to the crumbling and ebbing away of life and in doing this, discovered how it flows from the tangible, the articulate and the comprehensible to the intangible and the inscrutable. In the end, it's almost entirely an act of faith, or so it seemed to be to me.

Perhaps you, my reader, are slightly younger than me, just beginning the journey I've been on or, older, with both parents gone, still in the twilight zone of grief. I hope I can slide some useful information across the page about a variety of things: health-care directives and powers of attorney for personal and medical care; choosing a nursing home and the questions to ask; therapeutic touch and life review; the tell-tale signs of dementia and how to mitigate them; and the signs of impending death. But mostly I hope that in reading my story, you'll understand all that can be gained by daring to cross over: from being the good and dutiful caregiver slightly on the outside of the situation, to being an insider and intimate fellow traveller. I've only realized while writing this book how much I learned as I groped along, as I let intuition, love, and forgiveness guide me as I tried to be there, helping Mum find her way out of this world. For me, it was the last step in growing up.

Join me in my grieving journey. Let me join you in yours.

The Ground Begins to Shift

Ready to sew some voluptuous new fabric, I trawl the pale thread off the spool, channel it smoothly through the loop, and begin the tricky descent that will lodge it invisibly between the shiny chrome disks furnishing tension in my sewing machine. Then the world seems to tilt. I'm not sure where the thread goes next as a wave of grief engulfs me, the fact of Mum being dead nearly four years seemingly gone in a snap of the fingers. I start again, wondering if Mum herself did the same thing, remembering all those months when she had my sewing machine at her place to mend all those things that just piled up undone, and me impatiently muscling in to take over.

I draw out the thread once more, twist it down and through the tension disks, then up again toward the second loop. Maybe it was her arthritis and the general weak grip she felt at times, making it difficult to grasp and hold something as insubstantial as thread. It's taut now between my thumb and forefinger, and I hold it firm as I direct it through the intricate steps, twisting it around and up again to slide it inside the wire loop. Was it here that she had trouble, and was it her eyesight failing? Or was it her memory going blank halfway through the threading routine, a routine she knew by heart, for God's sake. What could have been simpler?

There had been hints, evidence of frustration in the balled-up bits of thread spewing from the pair of pants stuck in the machine where Mum was re-doing the seam, the thread having jammed before she'd managed even an inch.

"The machine won't work," she said once, and I immediately stepped in to fix it, as if that was the point, not the mishmash of tangled thread telling its tale, the tension near breaking point in Mum's voice. I take my time now, revisiting each step in this complicated fixture of a woman's world, for Mum's generation at least. I imagine her confusion, her determination, her rage. Perhaps she muttered "damn," the one swear word she ever allowed herself. Thread in hand, I let myself in on what she might have gone through, get a little closer to her there in the bursting silence of the sunroom in the cottage by the Rideau River where she lived alone for more than ten years after my father died.

I lean over to thread the sewing-machine needle itself, its tiny eye at the very tip. I blink, focusing on the hole, and through it I seem to catch a glimpse of my mother walking along the peak of the barn roof at the farm on a hot July day, wearing skimpy shorts and a halter-top, both splattered with roofing tar. She's carrying a bucket of tar in one hand and a dripping brush in the other, held away from her body to help her keep balance. She's also wearing bright red lipstick freshly applied before she climbed the ladder with Dad, at the top of which she cheerfully took over the bucket and brush, transferred to the makeshift ladder straddling the roof, climbed that and set off on her own, determined to patch the holes at the far end, insisting that she'd be perfectly safe. At one point, she paused in her careful walking, and waved the brush at us. "Halloo," she called. And of course we all waved back, craning our necks and smiling like crazy.

Though she was christened with the classic royal names, Elizabeth Anne, friends and family always called her "Beaver," a nickname bestowed on her as a toddler one day when her mother had taken her to someone's home for tea—"one of the Molsons," Mum always pointed out when telling the story. Mum would not sit still but spent the time crawling and pulling herself up on the various low tables, crammed with knick-knacks—no doubt, Limoges and Royal Doulton. The women watched as Mum lifted different ones in turn, and carefully set them back, never breaking a thing then moved on. "Busy as a beaver," the hostess said.

Mum had a rule. She told anyone who wanted to be her—Beaver's—friend that they had to promise always to do "what I want to do," she explained when telling another of her favourite stories. One day this involved playing hooky from school. This was in Sherbrooke, Quebec. In the 1920s, it was a lumber and mining town with a few small industries such as glove making and dairy. Horses were still used for daily deliveries of coal and wood for furnaces, and of bottled milk in the morning. Since Beaver loved horses, she took her new friend to a local livery stable where they fed the pastured draft horses bits of grass. They then roamed the patches of woods nearby, careful to stay out of sight of adults. When it was time for the school bell to ring, they wandered back toward school to join the scattering of home-bound children thinking this was easy. Her father, a McGill University–trained doctor who was struggling to establish a local rural practice during the Depression, called her into his office at the front of the house. He'd had a call from the school principle, he said. Beaver hadn't thought of that. She stood there aghast that her father might be displeased with her. Instantly subdued, she promised that she'd never play hooky again.

Most of Mum's stories were about her father, Dr. Douglas Bayne, whom she adored. In one, he had everyone in the household lined up for a diphtheria shot. The local woman who came in to cook started wailing and crying when the needle went into her arm. But when it was Mum's turn, she didn't make a sound. "I knew he was proud of me—not to make a fuss," she said. I don't know if this was before or after her mother died, suddenly, of a burst appendix when Mum was nine years old. Mum herself had nearly died of scarlet fever, and spent a year in bed in the months leading up to her mother's appendicitis—when mere sulpha drugs were no match for the septicemia that set in. Mum's world changed utterly that year. She not only lost her mother, she also lost her friend Evelyn Rider, the nineteen-year-old from a farm in Lac-Mégantic who had worked as live-in house help for three years, and had kept Mum company during her illness and long convalescence. Evelyn was sent away because it was thought improper to have a young woman in the house with the still-young widowed doctor. Instead, through the considerable connections of his late wife's Westmount family, a spinster friend of the family in England crossed the Atlantic and came to live with the family in the capacity of part governess, part housekeeper, and family friend. Her name was Jennifer Brumwell. A doctor's daughter herself, she had attended a Swiss finishing school, had studied to be an apothecary, and played the grand piano.

As she was being introduced to the children, the woman they were taught to call Aunt Jen took off her glove so that she could shake hands with them. Mum, telling the story nearly a lifetime later, recalled seeing the hand descending. "The fingers were white, like sausages. Sausages," Mum always added when telling this story. And then she stopped. I still don't know whether she stood her ground and took the outstretched hand, or bolted.

Years later when I was a young mother, I visited Aunt Jen, and quizzed her about those early years. She mostly remembered adventures, stories of being plunged for the first time in her life into the wilds of rural Quebec where Mum's father built a cabin at the head of a lake so remote there was no road, even when I was little. He built it as a family retreat, and Mum spent happy summers there as a youth, picking blueberries in the bush, canoeing with her younger brother Ron, and accompanying her father on hikes up the local mountain, which in the British grand expeditionary tradition he had named "Bayne's Bump." Still, Aunt Jen remembered one curious thing about the skinny, pale little Beaver from the months shortly after her arrival. That was her habit of hoarding bits of food in her room: slices of bread, a cupcake, and cookies. She hid these, often wrapped in a hankie, in the back of her dresser drawer in the bedroom she shared with her sister Marjorie. Aunt Jen routinely ferreted them out and threw them away. I gather that nothing was ever said, and that Mum's stashing of food eventually stopped.

For high school, Mum was sent to Montreal to attend Trafalgar School for Girls. Again, through family connections, it was arranged that she would board with her mother's family, the Youngers, in the three-storey home in Lower Westmount with bell pulls for the servants, red velvet curtains at windows and doorways, plus oak pocket doors opening onto the dark dining room and front parlour off the still-darker entrance hall. By then, the old patriarch, James Younger was dead, and Mum's Aunt Mildred, nicknamed "Muttie," was living there with her husband, a distant family cousin, and their son. Aunt Muttie was also strictly devout, subscribing to *The Daily Light*, and insisting on nothing but sacred texts for Sunday reading. So Mum arranged for a succession of friends to come and rescue her on Sunday afternoons.

After high school, Mum went to McGill University where she started pre-med thinking to follow her father's footsteps, but switched to arts because she couldn't imagine anyone going to a woman doctor. In her second year, she was drawn to a handsome, debonair but also gentle and kind man by the name of Donald Menzies. She also seized the occasion of the annual Sadie Hawkins' Dance, where the girls get to do the asking, to make his acquaintance. Still, making a commitment was something else. In the story I got partly from Dad, he chose to risk everything in the face of Mum's insistent "playing the field" and dating other men. He told her that if she didn't love him, they might as well stop seeing each other. And he resolutely stayed away. Eventually, Mum called him about going to see a movie, and he came to pick her up. Then, in the dark front hall at Aunt Muttie's house, as he helped her on with her coat, then watched her fuss over the buttons and scarf, he nudged her gently. Do you have something to tell me? Apparently, she then muttered into her coat, "I love you."

By then the war was on. They married on the eve of Dad's being sent away for training. When he was sent overseas, Mum carried on the tradition of using family connections, and got herself sent to London with the Red Cross. This was in the last months of the Blitz. London was in shambles, still besieged with robotized flying ordinances, called buzz bombs that flew low over the city until they ran out of fuel, stopped buzzing and dropped, exploding wherever they fell. Yet Mum was never afraid, even when one dropped in Hyde Park where she had been strolling with my father, on leave. Her favourite story, however, was the reputation she developed while helping out at night in a North London hospital when wounded soldiers regained consciousness after surgery. They often woke up thrashing, she explained, because they thought they were still on the beaches of Normandy, or storming the streets of Caen. So she would drape her body across theirs on the bed and put her head right next to their ear. As they surfaced, she whispered to them, "It's alright; you're safe. It's alright, you're safe," her lovely contralto voice soothing their still-shattered nerves, the sound of sirens outside the hospital window willed away. Of course, more than one recovering soldier developed a crush on her, she said when telling this story. But she just waved her wedding ring at them and carried on.

The war ended, and, in September, 1945, Dad was sent back to Canada with shrapnel from a mortar-shell hit still in his leg, and the memory of killing an enemy soldier still in his mind. His pre-war job at Imperial Tobacco Company's Canadian branch plant in Montreal was available if he wanted it back, which he did. Mum and Dad managed to rent a room as their first post-war home, and my brother Douglas was born in July 1946. He slept in a bureau drawer. A year later, Janet was born, and cradled in the second bureau drawer. Soon their savings, along with a Veterans' housing loan, were enough to build a house in Baie d'Urfé, a newly minted suburb on the west island of Montreal. When I was born, in June 1949, it was ready for occupancy.

Mum didn't fit the standard label of "stay-at-home mother," carving at least one career out for herself—two if you count the birds, three if you consider the garden, four if you count the farm. (The two-hundred acre property in eastern Ontario included a rundown house and barn, which had been abandoned after the war. My parents bought the acreage in lieu of a summer cottage thinking that caring for it and restoring its leeched and eroded soil could be a family project.) The activity that came closest to being a career, in that it made her money, was investing in the stock market. She generally did this in the winter months, when we didn't go to the farm, but stayed full time in Baie d'Urfé. Mum specialized in penny stocks that she read up about in the quiet that settled in after she'd got Dad off to the commuter train for work and then us kids up, fed with porridge and off to school with peanut butter and jelly sandwiches for lunch, and our homework in our arms. At that point, she made a pot of tea and took it upstairs to the master bedroom where she sat under the covers on her side of the bed, the tea tray on the nightstand beside her, reading the previous day's *Financial Post* and *Montreal Star*, which my father had brought home for her from the office. She sat there for an hour or so drinking cups of tea, discarding the news section, the women's section, and spreading the stock and investment pages across the vast empty space of the double bed. Then she got Beau on the phone, my father's friend who had also served overseas with the Black Watch in the war. But instead of asking his advice as a stockbroker, she simply told him what to buy and what to sell for the day. She was that confident, that bold; though clearing out her cupboards years later, I found a large brown envelope marked "Bust" where she stashed stock certificates on small mining companies in which she had kept faith even as they went under. Still, the envelope wasn't that full; Mum actually did rather well for herself over the years.

Phoning done, she got dressed, made the bed, brushed her luxuriant black hair, bundled and bobby pinned it in the rolled look that was fashionable in the forties, set the front roll into a wave with more bobby pins from the EB Eddy matchbox that she kept on a shelf in the medicine cabinet, then set herself to work on whatever main project she had planned for the day: laundry on Monday, ironing on Tuesday, and so on. There were always other things, especially seasonal gardening items on the to-do lists Mum made for herself on the back of envelopes. Things like "stake raspberries," "weed south bed," "mark zinnias" (for clipping as seed heads worth saving), or "glads" (gladiolas which, depending on the time of year meant either planting or taking up the bulbs that will die if left in the ground over winter). She never wrote down anything about birds and birdhouses, perhaps because these were her passions as opposed to chores. Late winter, I often came home from school to find her in the basement, sawing up bits of old barn board she salvaged for making birdhouses, getting ready for the swallows returning in early April. Over the years, she made hundreds of houses, each one painted white or dark forest green. However, her best, most fantastic creations, finished with elaborate perches and painted white with green trimming, were multi-layered, multi-holed "apartment" houses for her beloved martins. The largest in the swallow family, martins nest in colonies and have the delightful habit of bringing their fledglings back to the nest at night and noisily tucking them back into their proper home-hole. I'd come home from the ball park some evenings and find my parents sitting outside with an after-supper pot of coffee, their wooden lawn chairs drawn up side by side, watching the avian drama. I can remember sometimes also seeing my father's arm extending through the gap in the arm of Mum's chair, and I knew without looking that his fingers were laced with hers and that every so often they'd give each other's hand a little squeeze. Dad had a gift for intimacy, and Mum let him use it on her, certainly in moments like this. There would have been others too, lots of them, though they always seemed distant from the realm we children inhabited. We were Mum's daytime world, separate from the sphere she shared with Dad, whose time with us was mostly around going to church on Sundays while Mum stayed home for a bit of quiet time on her own. The crossover point during the week was when Mum changed out of her work clothes, put on a dress, stockings and heels, and removed the bobby pins from her wave-set ready for when Dad came home on the 6:15 train from the city. Whereupon Mum met him at the door, kissed him fulsomely on the mouth, and began setting the dining room table. By then Mum had usually fed us children supper, and sent us off either to bed, to finish our chores for the day if we hadn't gotten them done after school, or to do our homework while she and Dad had dinner and drank their coffee alone.

Still, I was good at tracking Mum, and slipping in next to her during the quiet moments of her day. When I was still too young to go to school, I often inveigled her into a game of hide-and-seek when she went upstairs to have tea in her bedroom, usually in the morning when she read the papers but sometimes too in the afternoon, when she treated herself to a chapter from the latest Perry Mason mystery Dad had brought home for her from the company's employee library.

When I was older and going to school, I was good at reading the feel of the house when I got home off the bus. Sometimes there was a particular stillness that told me I'd find Mum in bed with a migraine. Part of me hated for her to be sick. But the rest of me relaxed. It was safe for me to advance, to take some initiative even if was just to take care of her. I took off my shoes and made my stealthy approach up the stairs. The drapes in my parents' bedroom were usually drawn even if it was overcast and dull outside because any light was excruciating. My sock feet silent, I crept toward the bed, listening for Mum's breathing to judge if by some miracle she had drifted off to sleep. Usually she just lay there totally still, trying to keep the nausea down, sometimes giving a little groan, which was my signal to speak.

Whispering, I offered to freshen up the facecloth she used to ease the pain of the headache. "That would be nice," she murmured, handing it across to me, and giving my fingers a little squeeze. I remember how hot and dry the facecloth always was in my small and eager hand. Always I turned on the tap full blast, ran the water as cold as it would come so that I could make everything better in this miraculously transformed bit of cloth. The facecloth gently draped over Mum's hot forehead, I crept away, returning later offering a cup of tea. If she were really on the mend, I'd make a pot and join her in the bed, the fever heat of the sheets making me cozy and warm. By suppertime, she was usually up and dressed, the bed made up all smooth and wrinkle free, and that would be that.

When my father died, of lung cancer at sixty-eight, Mum didn't say a word. She didn't even want us by-then adult children around. By then too, we were all in households, careers, and families of our own, linked back to our old home orbit only by the rituals of occasional visits. Still, I sent Mum letter after letter trying to share my grief, to creep a hand close myself. She didn't write back. Actually, she told me later, she burned my letters—whether after she had read them or not, she never said, and I didn't dare to ask. She also stayed on alone at the winter home in Fort Myers Beach, that she and Dad had bought when he retired, and where they had played bridge, attended church together, and taken up Scottish country dancing. They hadn't been there long that late fall when Dad's cancer took a turn for the worse and he died. Come spring, Mum came north again, resolved to stay on alone at the farm, to which they had moved after Dad retired and they sold their home in Baie d'Urfé. Unfortunately, its quarter-mile laneway made it almost inaccessible in winter. I arrived at the farm one day to find Mum on the tractor in one of the back fields plagued with stones, crab grass, and thistles. She had the spring-tooth harrow hitched on the back, and was going after the weeds with a vengeance. I stood and watched her tear up and down the field, the harrow almost bouncing out of the ground, a cloud of dust rising furiously in the air. It was the closest thing to grieving that I ever saw.

Even when she broke her arm, she carried on. Well, she managed this because the neighbour, Jean-Guy Bourcier, dropped by almost daily to help and keep an eye on her. Plus, I upped my visits to once a week, driving the hour and a half each way to brush her hair, make meals, fill up the wood box. She had me take a picture of her shucking a cob of corn, using her foot to anchor the cob while she used her one good hand to strip the husk away. In the picture, she's smiling triumphantly, clearly demonstrating how much she can do for herself, dauntless and brave. If anything, Dad's death had made her even more this way: cheerfully, stubbornly self-sufficient. And we adult children left her to it, carrying on with our own busy lives. By then, Doug was a partner in a law firm and ran a bank on the side, while also raising four sons and tending flower gardens at both his Ottawa home and a cottage in West Quebec. Janet worked as a senior manager for Edmonton Telephones and, in her second marriage, was learning to be a step-mother to two nearly grown boys. Dick, the youngest, was a doctor, and combined a busy career in hospital administration, international tuberculosis research and clinical practice with being an active father to his two daughters. Like Doug, I lived in Ottawa, and was almost as busy, with a mix of teaching part time at Carleton University, researching and writing books, plus speaking at national and sometimes international conferences. I also had my own household to run, a large vegetable and flower garden, a husband and a pre-teen son on whom I doted. Still, after Dad died, I made it my business to do the hour-and-a-half drive to the farm and back at least once a month, just to check in, to see if there was anything I could do. And gradually, between the upkeep and living there alone, the farm got to be too much, and between my sister Jan's blunt suggestion that it was time to pass it on to Dick, who was to inherit it, and my gently encouraging her to move closer to Ottawa, we got Mum moved to a run-down old cottage on the Rideau River, twenty minutes' drive from my home.

A cottage was sufficient because Mum carried on driving down to Florida in the fall, back again in the spring, and by all appearances she would continue doing this and everything else in her busy life forever. It was a shock, then, when Mum developed pneumonia in her late seventies and nearly died. She had gone down to Florida as usual, pooh-poohing all the while that she was sick despite the clear evidence that she was. Dick, the doctor, arranged to have Mum medevaced back to Canada, and after a few anxious days, with tubes and wires all around her frail and waxen body, she pulled through. I brought her home to where I then lived with my husband Miles and son Donald, pleased and proud to care for her during her convalescence. Then, when she insisted she was well enough, I flew down to Florida with her, to help get her settled, but hoping to bask in the sun a bit too, my just deserts for all I'd done.

Almost immediately, she arranged to hold the neighbourhood dinner party that her illness had forced her to cancel, and I spent a busy time helping to make that happen. When the guests arrived, I watched Mum emerge from her bedroom where she'd gone well over an hour earlier to get changed. She'd put on the gorgeous floor-length red velvet dinner gown she always wore for the annual event she and Dad used to host. She'd put on the flashy jewellery she normally wore with it, setting off the deep décolletage. And she'd plastered her mouth with her usual bright red lipstick, so much that some was on her upper teeth.

She looked grotesque, her face so sickly pale against the red dress and lipstick. Her body, now shrunken by illness, was incapable of filling out the gown, which sagged from her shoulders and breasts. Looking back, what I see now is a magnificent and moving sight: a gutsy determined woman rising to the occasion, greeting her guests with all the energy and charm she could muster, the lipstick on her tooth also a sign of how much of a front Mum was putting on, revealing as it did how weak and trembling her hand still was in applying her staple piece of makeup. I felt no empathy at the time, however, only resentment as Mum kicked away all the traces of how much I was propping her up. She never acknowledged what I'd been doing for her, and I sat there at the far end of the table, feeling invisible because she wouldn't. I stayed stuck like that, miserable and angry, for the duration of the dinner, unable to share Mum's moment of returning glory, unable to receive the warmth of her assembled friends and neighbours, some of whom would have seen or heard the ambulance, and possibly been afraid for themselves.

A couple of years later, she developed congestive heart failure and chose a high-risk surgery rather than a slow crippling of her life through shortness of breath. If she could get back to gardening, she told the surgeon who read her the risk stats, taking the chance was worth it. "I've had a good life. I'm ready to die," she told me the night before the surgery. Sure I thought, because neither of us believed it; she looked indomitable as always. She scrubbed herself vigorously with the pre-surgery antibacterial soap, her eyes dancing with excitement at the imminent adventure. And sure enough, she bounced back from this health crisis too, and soon she was back to her garden, as planned. Yet the weeds started to make inroads, not immediately around the house, but in the border beds. She could in fact do less and less; the crab grass was the first to notice.

I did notice that she was repeating herself more than she used to do. She was forgetting the odd word or where she'd put something away. But she brushed it off if I asked her about it, saying she was just tired, and I let it go, her word as always trumping my sense of things. One day, though, I was outside finishing off some weeding while she started supper. She came out the back door to say: "You know, it's the funniest thing. How do I make lemon-meringue pie? I can't seem to remember." I was shocked. But just as quickly, I moved to reassure her, telling her I'd be right in. We'd do it together. That would be nice. A few weeks later, Mum called me on the phone wanting to know where the applesauce maker was.

"It'll be in the same place. I just don't know where that place is!" she said. I told her where to look, and didn't hear back, so I assumed that all was well and I, feeling relieved and reprieved as well, carried on with my life.

Another day, we'd been hanging birdhouses. When we finished, I volunteered to put the stepladder away. "No, no, I'll do it," she insisted, and hoisted the thing as if she was as strong as ever. I watched to make sure she could manage, and sure enough she carried it across the lawn. Then she hesitated, and instead of carrying on toward the shed, she turned toward the house. She walked up the back steps, opened the door, and carried the ladder into the house. There had been other things going amiss or missing. But this was different, so startlingly out of joint with all that's normal and expected that I can see it still: Mum matter-of-factly carrying the stepladder into the house and setting it against the wall in the living room as if this was perfectly normal. But it wasn't. Mum was becoming displaced much as people become displaced in wartime when soldiers and bombs overrun their homes, turning them into rubble. Only here, Mum was being displaced from her home in her own home. She was being displaced from herself, yet carrying on as though she was still on the barn roof.

In a way too, I was still the little girl down below: Mum's faithful cheerleader, plus her helper and informal, if unacknowledged, caregiver. I was unprepared to take the initiative, unequipped to say: Mum, time to come down now. Time to make a shift. Nor was I one to take the lead in the family, to take charge. My older siblings were: Doug the lawyer looked after Mum's legal stuff; Jan the business manager and executor of our parents' wills, looked after Mum's financial stuff; and then there was Dick, to whom we all looked concerning medical matters. If I had a role at all, it was as messenger: the one who kept track, who passed on stories. Generally too, I deferred, certainly to Mum but also to the others and their confident decisiveness.

In a sense too, though Mum was eighty and I nearly fifty, I was stuck at one end of a teeter-totter in how Mum and I related to each other: she talking, me listening, she doing her thing, me accommodating and going along. Now, her end of the seesaw was falling apart. I would go flying.

Looking back, the sight of Mum calmly putting the stepladder away in the living room was like an earthquake breaking the Richter scale. Things weren't as they used to be; they never would be again. I was being displaced as much as Mum was. Yet nothing of that registered on the page of my journal where I recorded the incident, along with all the other small seemingly defining signs of Mum's decline. I did it coolly, like the reporter I used to be:

focused on the facts, only the facts, keeping myself and my own emotions out of the picture. It was the only way I could cope.

I also focused on making the case to my siblings that Mum should move into a seniors' residence before some calamity struck, and the ladder incident was more hard evidence that things couldn't continue. Mum was getting frail, not eating properly, not looking after herself, or keeping up with basic housekeeping. She couldn't carry on living on her own, no matter what she said, and regardless of how brusquely she said it, not just to me but to the others as well. Perhaps I wasn't the only one still gawking at Mum way up there on the barn roof, mesmerized by her daring, defying even gravity.

For the most part, I think I was just putting in time, waiting for something to happen that would take things out of my hands. Meanwhile, I focused on doable things, like getting her to eat more nutritiously, and navigating the chaos as things piled up. The kitchen counter had always been cluttered, lined at the back with stacks of used paper napkins, including bib-sized ones saved from an all-you-can eat restaurant where Mum and Dad used to dine during their winters together in Florida. Mum's were identifiable by the slight crescent of red lipstick, a mark too of her habit of dabbing her lips, lady-like, rather than wiping them when eating. Fifteen years after Dad's death, forty or fifty of these still teetered at the back of the counter, slightly yellowed and covered with dust, surrounded by fly specks and even the odd dropping from the mice that invaded the place when Mum was away for the winter. Over the years, I'd grown used to the sight of these napkins as they became merely the backdrop to an escalating accumulation of junk: a cracked bud vase filled to overflowing with used twist ties, a broken saucer filling up with sugar satchels Mum snuck into her purse from the restaurants Doug took her to for dinner, her hoarding instincts from childhood resurfacing, perhaps, reinforcing her instincts to save what she could. There was a salt shaker needing to be filled, a mouse trap coming apart on one side, and, more recently, the nozzle from the sprayer she used to dose her raspberry canes with pesticide.

I tried to keep a little space clear and clean so I could chop vegetables for supper, or roll out pastry for a pie. I tidied up the piles and even pushed things farther back when Mum wasn't looking. Once I grabbed up a handful of the useless napkins. "Can't we throw some of these out at least?" I asked, hearing the whine in my voice, the piles of things unsaid inside me.

"Just leave them," she said, taking the mess from my hands.

Months later, Mum still had the sewing machine out on the card table she'd set up in the sun porch, because she hadn't sewn up her jeans. Now the sofa cover was there, a row of pins along a seam that had simply worn out with hard use. I tried to do the sewing myself, but Mum wouldn't have it. "Just leave it; I'll do it later," she said, and put on the kettle for tea.

Things Mum baked were increasingly coming out of the oven burned because she'd forgotten them, or flat because she'd forgotten to add the baking powder. I brought more, and baked more. I also brought whole meals in Tupperware containers, which she simply needed to heat up in the microwave. One day, Mum put one of these containers into the oven. The plastic melted, and began to drip from the rack. Luckily, the smell alerted us, and we managed to turn off the oven before the plastic burst into flames.

I cleaned more and re-washed dishes that increasingly were stacked on the shelf with bits of dried food stuck to the plates, or a veil of grease on a glass. I bullied Mum to change her clothes, to wash her hair when it began to smell.

Visit after visit, I did what I could before letting her sideline it all with another pot of tea. I wasn't ignoring the larger picture, just not seeing it, and rendered helpless in the face of Mum's insistent carrying on. She was fine, and she ate very well, you know. She not only said this to me, but also to Janet and Dick when they phoned to inquire, and probably to Doug too when he took her home for Sunday supper. Visit after visit, my energy drained away beneath the familiar rhythms of Mum making tea, and urging me to have another cup.

On the day of the displaced stepladder, I focused on making pastry for the pie Mum always liked to have for dessert because, I knew, it made the meal special that way, more like a little dinner party than just another supper. I'd even brought my own shortening to ensure the pastry was fresh. After giving the countertop mess a violent shove (flyspecks and mouse turds be damned), I'd laid everything out on the counter when Mum came back from the bathroom.

"What are you doing?" she asked as she came around the counter. I duly explained what was perfectly obvious to us both: I was making pastry.

"I still have some," she said, and fetched her pastry out from the back of the fridge where I knew full well it still sat, a grey lump that she'd made at least two months ago, using congealed grease from the roasting pan and more water than the pastry could handle with any hope of being flaky.

"It's okay; save it for another time when I'm not here," I said looking at the horrid little ball. I didn't even want to touch it, let alone try to roll it out.

I turned back to what, after all, I had already started.

"Don't be silly," she said. Stepping forward, she grabbed up the sieve, already filled with the requisite two cups of flour and half a teaspoon of salt, and dumped it back into the flour canister. Whether she had forgotten that a sieve will sieve or she didn't care at that point, I'll never know. I just remember the flour drifting like a length of sheer curtain in the wake of her furious motion. She was immediately flustered and annoyed. "How stupid of me," she said. She started to whisk up the spilled flour, wanting to put that in the canister too. Her voice sounded tight, as though she was on the verge of tears.

"It's okay," I said, moving to clean up the mess, to smooth the situation over, ignoring her tone of voice, or immediately trying to cover it up. I plugged in the kettle for tea, which we took outside, well away from the site of the crisis. Mum chatted away about the usual things she talked about, and I went along.

2

The Diagnosis

We should all have been braced for Mum getting Alzheimer's because her father had gone down with it. His memory ran backward, and so he forgot his second wife Margaret and the children from his second marriage before he forgot people like Mum, progeny of the first. That must have been hard enough for that second family, and even more so when Mum never went for a visit. "I'd rather remember him the way he was," was all she'd say. Though that didn't stop the stories, passed around like a terrible secret from phone call to phone call, about how Granddad had yelled at Margaret, a long-time nurse at the hospital where Granddad, a doctor, had practiced, now trying to take care of him at home. How he hit her once, in the months before Margaret finally placed him in a home. How he'd given away his prized stamp collection to a man who came by the house selling life insurance policies, though he'd promised it to his son, my uncle. How his teenaged daughters, Susan and Catherine, didn't dare bring anyone home from school in case their seventy-five-year-old father said or did something awful.

Was Mum on the verge of something awful too? Was she getting Alzheimer's? The prospect terrified me: the mad woman in the attic, the door locked and me alone in there with her, trapped and unable even to scream. That's what I was afraid of, so afraid that I couldn't look Alzheimer's in the eye. I didn't even contact the Alzheimer's Society until after Mum was dead. At the time, too, the fear was for myself: wanting to protect myself against Mum, and the possibility of her lashing out at me. That's what defined the disease in my ignorant mind, not the sad unravelling of a daily existence: the difficulty in remembering one's own telephone number, the names of old friends and family suddenly beyond one's reach.

One day we were having tea outside on the lawn beside the river, watching the bird traffic over the water. The resident kingfisher flew off its favourite dead branch of the maple tree at the water's edge, shrieking raucously.

"What's that bird?" Mum asked.

"Kingfisher," I said, shocked because my mother was known as "the bird woman." She knew the names of all the local breeds and the most intimate details of their nesting routines. Now, it was as though someone was splashing whiteout across Mum's brain; she could no longer read even the well-thumbed pages of her memory.

A month or so later, again outside having tea by the water, she asked, "What's that flying insect that hops?"

"A grasshopper," I said. Again, I wrote this down in my journal for future reference, along with the stepladder incident and the forgotten recipe for pie. I felt better at having done so, facing up to it sort of, but leaving it at that. Yet, as I learned later, these were classic signs of the mild to moderate stages of Alzheimer's disease. Mum had it already.

I did speak to my siblings about it. In fact it was my hope that they'd rescue me, taking the issue out of my hands so I wouldn't be the one to blame for putting Mum into a home against her will. In one journal entry, I even made a note to call my sister and brother. It was August, 1999. I'd returned from some out-of-town speaking engagement, and dropped into Mum's place just to check in, do a little cleaning if I could, and ensure that she had supper on the go before I headed to my own home and family circle. I arrived to find her confused and dishevelled. Her hair was falling loose from where she normally kept it bobby pinned neatly in place around the top of her head. "Oh, is it Tuesday?" she asked. "What happened to Monday?" She couldn't follow a train of thought without veering off onto another topic. She couldn't remember people's names, and explained that "when you don't actually hold the nameplate, when you aren't actually there, you know?" I phoned home to say I was staying the night, and Mum slowly seemed to regain her bearings as I set the meal on the table, put away the clothes she'd left just outside the bathroom, and brought her life back to normal. Over breakfast in bed the next morning, she said, "There was a time, you know? I can't remember when it was. Everything was pitch black, and I didn't know where I was. I called out for you, but I didn't get any answer. So I just subsided." After recording all this in my journal, I wrote: "Has she had a mini-stroke, I wonder. I'll call Dick tonight, I think. Then Jan."

When I asked Jan whether because of Granddad, she worried that Mum might get Alzheimer's too, she said that Granddad's illness had never seemed very real to her, because we never saw him when he was sick. When I spoke to Dick, he said that from the time I called him a year or so ago, he'd been thinking it was dementia caused by mini-strokes, not Alzheimer's, and linked with Mum's chronic high blood pressure. I shied away from speaking to Doug, I think, because I had an inkling of what his position might be. As he told me later, he welcomed any sign of Alzheimer's in Mum, "because it weakened my enemy." For the longest time, he had taken an almost vicious pride in declaring Mum as his enemy, the two of them locked in mortal combat, with no hope of reconciliation.

In a way we were still stuck as a family. Our neighbour at the farm, Jean-Guy, unabashedly referred to Mum simply as "the boss," but with such an accepting smile on his face that I was amazed. Growing up with this was different, and tended to polarize us as children: not just competing against each other for Mum's approval and attention but, later, lining up as either against her for all the ways she had denied us, controlled us, disciplined and judged us or, in the other camp, fully on her side, loyal no matter what. It made for uneasy relations among us children as adults, Mum's presence a force to be reckoned with even when she was nowhere in sight.

No surprise then that the family took a dim view of making a fuss, and yet I had a reputation as the one who did, "poor thing." I was the emotional one, which by implication meant the weak one. Plus, my inclination to take care of Mum was suspect. Doug once told me bluntly that I was wasting my time chasing after Mum's love, and should align myself with him, which as his champion since childhood, I had originally tended to do. When I turned to Jan in Edmonton, pointing out how much Mum was slipping, how much I had to do for her because Mum was increasingly incapable of doing things for herself, she reminded me that "well, you do need to be needed." She wasn't being unkind, just sticking to being the matter-of-fact one in the family. Plus, I imagine that's how she saw things, as a continuation of me taking on too much, whining a little because it wasn't duly noticed and appreciated. And I have to admit, that was me alright, at the start of this: still the eager-to-please little girl. The fact that Mum really did need help, and was more and more lost without it, was easily missed, especially since Mum herself was still denying it, and it must have been easier to maintain a façade of competence on the phone long distance. I didn't argue. Jan was in Alberta and I was the daughter who lived close by.

Weeks and months went by, and I did what I could, keeping a low profile, and making notes in my journal, accumulating evidence of Mum's steady decline. One day, she phoned to ask where the post office was. It's inside the general store in Kars, the village just up the road, I reminded her, wondering how she could forget something as simple as that. "I visualize things, but sometimes the visual doesn't come up too clearly," she said. Some time later, she drove farther afield, into the nearby town of Manotick to get groceries. She stopped at the Kars general store going home, and sought out Diana, the gracious Englishwoman who runs the post office at the back of the cluttered store. According to Diana, one of a few people who kept their eye on Mum and kept me at least a little informed on what was happening, Mum leaned in close and whispered, "Do you know where I live?" I think now, how sad, hopelessly lost within a mile of home! Yet all I remember feeling at the time was embarrassed, as though I was responsible. I should have known enough to prevent this sort of thing from happening.

"You'd think I'd know those three letterboxes," Mum said when she told me this story, referring to the cluster of rural mailboxes at the head of the lane, her house a short run down its length. Clearly she was annoyed with herself, and puzzled at why this familiar landmark was no longer familiar. "But I didn't recognize them," she said.

Now that I've delved into it, I can understand what was going on. It's not that Mum didn't recognize the mailboxes. Some part of her did recognize them. Rather, she couldn't place them in context. They were just free-floating signs to her, familiar and yet severed from the larger memory maps in her mind that would tell her why they were familiar, and how they related to getting from points A to B in the car. Now the landscape that had signified "close to home" was just more undifferentiated landscape: terra incognita. Plus, with her short-term memory shorting out, she was less able to stay focused on interpreting the signs. Everything that should have remained background noise, unnoticed, now clamoured for her attention as a possible clue. And I by and large left her there, floundering away. Unbeknownst to me, Mum had already progressed to stages 3 and 4 on the Global Deterioration Scale (GDS) of the disease. She didn't just have a problem remembering words and names (anomia), she was having trouble articulating and making sense of language and signs (aphasia) and even too, coordinating actions like driving and making meals (apraxia).

When the dementia is diagnosed, preferably in the early stages, doctors now routinely refer both patients and their caregivers to a local Alzheimer Society for inclusion in its First Link program, which provides useful background on what dementia involves, and what to expect. Most importantly, though, it offers counselling and self-help groups for both patient and caregiving family members. As Marg Eisner, director of programs and services at the Alzheimer's Society of Ottawa and Renfrew County explained to me: "Alzheimer's is a disease of losses, and in the early stages at least the people involved know what is going on. If they have a chance to talk, they can grieve. In fact, it's in facing the reality by talking about it that the grieving can begin."

Looking back through my journal, I can see hints of Mum admitting her sense of losing it. Once, I noted her saying, "I'm very stupid about these things. I know you'd like to know and

I'd like to tell you in exact terms, but..." There were clear signs of distress too, perhaps even some reaching out, as difficult as that would have been for someone as fiercely independent as Mum. "I feel a tightness inside, from all the running around. I feel lost inside myself," I recorded her having told me once. Not a word at how I responded, or how tight inside, how lost, I might have been feeling myself. Another time, on the phone, she told me, "I think I'm going downhill. I find if things don't work out, I get upset. I feel peculiar."

I didn't say a thing, didn't give Mum a chance to open up, to let us both in on what "peculiar" felt like, riding out the fear at what this meant as we named it and expressed it: the horror of her tumbling off the barn roof, the barn disintegrating, the ground cracking open under our feet.

People talk about paradigm shifts and tipping points as if it's just a matter of evidence accumulating in a scale that tips effortlessly across the dispassionate centre of the fulcrum. The scale comes down, and, bang, you realize: she's sick; she has Alzheimer's. Or it's like in a chemistry lab when you add enough sodium chloride to a solution and suddenly it resolves into crystals. Perhaps that is how things are when you're the scientist merely adding things to the beaker, but not when you're inside the glass container, part of the brew that is a lifetime of being, nested in relations that flow and flex a certain way. Perhaps the molecules in the solution put up a fight, not wanting to change, to take on this new crystal shape, no matter how elegant and improved, how reasonable and even appropriate to the changed situation. They might dislike, even rage at, their increasingly turgid liquid state, so to speak. But being in that pattern, relating monad to monad as a liquid, not a solid, is deeply familiar and there's comfort in that. Perhaps too, they're so immersed in the minutia, the matrix of atoms, the ongoing tension of protons and dancing electrons, that they can't even tell when a shift has taken place. I think this was part of it: Mum being in charge was all we knew, even when it was clear she no longer was.

Between that and wanting someone else to take charge and my own shrinking away from the fullness of what was happening, I did nothing. No, I did more and more, trying to take over more and more, mitigating disaster. I ran myself ragged, so much so that Mum was becoming a strain in my marriage; Miles angry at how much Mum expected of me, and took me for granted. "Monster," he called her once, though I think this was more a deflection of his accumulating anger toward me, and our faltering relationship. Still, some part of me felt better, my frustration vindicated, my resentment appeased by sleight of hand, which kept me going, and focused too on doing more good deeds, getting more tired and depressed as Mum forgot to clean the kitchen sink and bathroom, or to finish the job once she'd started. When I phoned to say I was coming for a visit, she'd often announce that "I might just defrost the fridge" then leave it for me to do the work. She also started taking things from my place—small items like gloves and a scarf. At her own house, she misplaced more and more things as well, and sometimes even thought that I'd taken them—her favourite pearl earrings, for example—when I suspect that she'd hidden them in what I sensed to be an increasing paranoia.

One day there was a curious scrape under the front bumper of Mum's car; she'd driven right over a concrete barrier. "What's this?" I asked, though when she laughed it off, I reasoned that it was minor enough that I could just laugh it off too. Another day the phone rang, and a woman wanted to know if I was Anne Menzies' daughter. She then wanted to confirm my address, for she proposed to drive in her own car, leading Mum back across town to where she was supposed to have turned. When they arrived, Mum took charge of the situation, graciously introducing this woman to me as if they were old friends back from an outing. She insisted too that the woman come to visit her and have a cup of tea and, on extracting a promise, waved fondly as the woman drove away.

"That was kind of her," I offered.

"I would have found my own way easily enough," she retorted. "Some people just like to be helpful, so I went along."

"Bullshit" went through me like a flare, and was as quickly snuffed out. I muttered something inane to get us past the awkward moment and, later, drew the first of the many maps I made for Mum over the next few months, this one laying out the route from Mum's place on the Rideau River to my house on the outskirts of Ottawa. I also drew a map that would take her to Doug's house closer into town. I suggested that Mum keep these maps in her glove compartment, and it worked for a while. But then, she either forgot they were there, or else even these simplified markings communicated less and less to her over time. By the time she couldn't recognize the mailboxes at the top of her own lane, she had a glove compartment full of these maps, some of them wrinkled from being crushed, even balled up as though in a fist.

Once, it was ten o'clock at night when she left Doug's place, and she got lost going home. Then, when she went to turn around, she backed up into a shallow ditch and got stuck there. She did what she usually did under the circumstances. She marched boldly up to the nearest house and asked for help. By the time she returned to her car, her purse had been stolen, along with her shoe bag in which she had tucked her good jewellery for safekeeping. She never admitted this, pooh-poohed the tufts of grass lodged in the wheel well and, later, complained to me several times in a tone that bordered on the vicious that she thought Doug must have taken her jewellery. She didn't say "stolen," but the way her voice came down hard on "taken" implied this, and I cringed.

The poet Emily Dickinson wrote famously that writers conjure an authentic sense of life by "telling it slant." And it occurs to me that it's how most of us live our lives: We cope by getting on with the ordinary practical things that need to be done, and only glance at the hard stuff since it's more bearable to come at it slant, sidling up to it. I'd like to say that I did it well, but I didn't. My inner sense of things, my intuition, was tracking Mum's imploding life beneath the bluster of her cover-ups and denials, and the accumulating chaos on the counter, in the sunroom . . . everywhere. Yet my outer self kept on with the normal routines, numb, dumb, and totally incapable of decisive action.

Still, the day Mum insisted on taking a turn at driving when I took her to Hamilton to see her brother Ron, I had the sense to seize the moment when she handed me irrefutable proof that there was something seriously wrong. She kept veering off onto the shoulder, and not seeming to notice the fifty-kilometre-speed-limit signs as we approached a town. When I told her to turn left, she didn't seem to know left from right. But the worst was her not seeming to notice other vehicles on the road. Once she veered across the mid-line with a truck approaching so close I had to yank the wheel to get her moved over fast enough. I was a wreck by the time I called a halt for gas. But I had my case. In the washroom, I jotted everything down on a piece of paper in my purse. Details to tell her doctor, who had the power, I'd learned from a friend, to have Mum's licence yanked out from under her. It wasn't exactly belling the cat, which getting her into a home had become in my mind. But at least I needn't worry about the trouble she could get into as she stopped at whatever house took her fancy whenever she got lost. Or if she got into a serious accident and was sued or, worse yet, killed someone.

I arranged with the doctor that I could accompany Mum into the examining room. Mum wasn't happy about this, but was too polite to say anything in public. The doctor gave me the opening: Any other concerns? And I told her about the driving. Mum immediately said: "I'm a very good driver. I've always been a good driver."

The doctor agreed wholeheartedly, nodding and smiling until Mum had finished. Then she raised the subject of a "geriatric assessment." Just to make sure that everything was fine. And somehow between the two of us, we kept the idea alive until it was agreed. The doctor would make the referral and I, the appointment. On the appointed day, I picked Mum up and drove her to the Élizabeth Bruyère Hospital, an old pale square-stoned institution with lighting that bleaches and flattens every face that enters. I remember the woman coming to take Mum into the room where she'd answer the various questions that would assess her "cognitive function." Mum stood up as straight as the osteoporosis she would never admit to permitted, clasped her elbows to her sides, purse clutched under one arm, and walked smartly across the waiting room, the metal tips of her high heels clicking loudly.

Was it the same day or did we come back for the results? I can't remember, only that the whole affair seemed to happen very fast, from assessment to diagnosis. Verdict. The geriatric specialist invited me into the consulting room with Mum, and gestured to a chair to the side of the two set up for them. Being included, being acknowledged as a primary caregiver, was still a novelty then, and I remember being pleased—smug even—as I sat down. There wasn't a desk between Mum and the doctor, only a small table, innocuous as a bedside stand. Just large enough for the manila folder that contained the test results. The doctor sat down opposite Mum, far enough that her crossed knees didn't touch Mum's, yet close enough that when she leaned forward to speak, her face was very near.

I waited as she leaned forward, the epitome of professional solicitude. I had worked toward this moment for so long, managed events through the doctor's protocols to conceal my hand in it, to hide behind the increasingly strict regulations about seniors' dangerous driving. I was feeling relieved. The necessary decisions were being taken out of my hands. I'd held up really rather well, I thought, looking after Mum as she became more and more difficult. Doctors were objectively making the case. This being so, the results would be irrefutable, beyond anyone's power to change. My brothers and sister would listen.

Everything was poised to fall into place. From my perch at the side of the room, I waited for the doctor to speak, and sure enough, she pronounced the A word. "The tests indicate probable Alzheimer's," she said. She mentioned a new medication, Aricept, that showed promise to slow the process. We can get you into the trial.... Meanwhile, she went on, she'd be writing to the Ministry of Transport. Mum wouldn't be able to drive anymore.

Mum had been wearing a polite smile all through this professional speech. Now I watched as the smile became stuck. Her whole face became rigid, mask-like, a caricature of a smiling face. Her hands were clasped in her lap, and I watched as her grip on herself tightened. She straightened herself in the chair. It was as though she was summoning all the poise and *savoir faire* that had carried her so successfully through her life till then.

When she spoke her voice was a paragon of sweet reason. Her diction was perfect. "How can you know I'm not a good driver?" she began, and immediately offered to take this woman out for a drive, to show her. The doctor smiled, her hand reaching to pull the manila folder closer.

Mum was wearing slacks that day, a pair I'd worn in my early twenties and had passed along to her when I gained weight in my thirties. I'd passed them on not because Mum couldn't afford to buy herself clothes, but because she wouldn't spend the money, and these were at least better than what she'd otherwise put on to go out. They were narrow in the pant leg and I noticed how thin Mum had become as she crossed her legs tighter and tighter, so tight that she twisted the crossed-over leg completely around the other one, pretzel like, and tucked her foot in behind its ankle. She was a small, shrivelled and shrunken old woman with an out-of-date hairdo and out-of-date shoes, and still she persisted. She kept her eyes fixed on the doctor's face. Mum had always trusted the personal approach; it had always served her well. She asked again, how could things she'd written down on a piece of paper indicate how well she could drive on the road? She was a good driver; she'd always been a good driver, she repeated. The doctor's expression didn't change. Only her hand moved, pulling the manila folder closer, opening it up: the evidence. The hard, objective evidence.

Instantly I hated her. Instantly I switched sides. The psychiatrist or neurologist, whoever she was, she was the authority figure, the one in charge. She was wearing a long grey wool dress that buttoned all the way up to her neck. Withholding, I thought, cruelly controlling from behind this front of professional pale-grey empathy. A person who looked at drawings old people had made of clocks, and came to rigid conclusions about them.

All the way home, Mum talked only about her driver's licence. Once she'd told me with no sense of irony: "I've always been in the driver's seat in my life." And I laughed out loud. So true, so true. She'd also been part of a tiny minority of women of her generation who drove the car even when with their husbands. For as long as I can remember, Mum always drove. Dad sometimes suggested mildly that she might slow down, and once she did get a speeding ticket. It was the only time I can remember her faltering: when she had to go to court. For some reason, she took us children along with her. For moral support? To sway the judge perhaps; she was that smooth, even sly when it came to getting her way. When they called her name and she stood up to say "yes," the word came out weak and wobbly. I can still remember my shock. It was my first inkling that Mum could be afraid.

Mum had rallied by the time we got back to her place, and focused exclusively on the appeal process the doctor had mentioned at the end. She'd take a new driver's test in the spring, she said, and meanwhile, I should go out on the road with her, give her some pointers. I nodded, seeming to go along with this, watching her hand clench and unclench itself into a fist on the table. In fact, I hoped everything might have been taken care of by then. Diagnosis in hand, I could convince my siblings that it was time for Mum to move into a seniors residence where, it was my thought, others could deal with whatever wallop the disease had yet to deliver. The fact that Dick didn't really agree with the "probable Alzheimer's" verdict, preferring the dementia label instead, was merely one more reason for me to ignore the literature on Alzheimer's that the doctor had given us, ignoring what it had to teach me.

I only pursued it after Mum died, wanting to fully understand what happens neurologically as Alzheimer's starts destroying the mind. I made an appointment to meet with Dr. Inge Loy-English, the hospital's memory disorder clinic's director, and she explained that the build-up of toxic beta-amyloid begins in the hippocampus, which takes new information coming in through the senses as short-term memory, and sends it to the cortex both for retaining it along with other experience as episodic memory and for interconnecting it with semantic memory's store of understood concepts to interpret and coordinate response. As that back-and-forth action starts to fail, people have trouble retrieving the word they want to say, or the name of something like an apple or a bird (anomia). They also have trouble with orientation, particularly with abstract things like an analog clock, which is why everyone tested at the clinic is asked to draw one. I remember the clock face that Mum drew. The hands were boldly drawn, and marked the time at ten after two, but the numbers were mostly bunched up at the top of the picture.

But why attach so much importance to the proper drawing of the clock, I wondered. I know that the clock is in fact an intensely layered set of abstractions, starting with the very idea of rendering living, breathing time as numbers arbitrarily set down around a circle. That's precisely why it lends itself to checking someone's planning or "executive" function, Dr. Loy-English explained. First, the people being tested have to plan how they will draw the clock, then how to sequence the numbers around the circle, and finally they must accurately place the hour and minute hands to indicate the correct time. It's not like getting someone to peel a potato, where the sequence unfolds with the physical action, and the action is vested in the hands. Here, it's all abstractions. The hand holding the pencil has to pull everything out of the mind.

Quite apart from drawing clocks, the sense of time passing is also lost, the doctor explained. Apart from not keeping track of time, and missing appointments, this affects the ability to focus, to grasp the interconnections of things, to follow a conversation or even a sequence in what had been familiar tasks—like making pastry. So it's not just memory, it's also memory management, the executive planning and coordinating function of the cortex, that breaks down. As the plaques spread throughout the cortex, more and more stored memories get walled off, and the semantic stuff of ideas and understanding disappears. This makes communication increasingly difficult (aphasia). At this point, "agnosia" sets in, which is the inability to make new knowledge out of old, to make the connections. And so you see a fork, but can't remember what it's used for. You see three mailboxes at the end of a lane, but don't know that they signal home. You see a traffic light that's just turned red, yet don't know that this means, "stop." But with short-term memory loss too, Dr. Loy-English said, you're not even aware of the difficulties you're having. Nor can you remember them, so you can't really judge your situation either. "Your own personal narrative is going to be very disjointed. Or even gone."

I told the doctor what I'd written in my journal, my sense of Mum becoming a displaced person, displaced from herself. Well, the doctor said, "She would have been constantly in the present, only the present. So, yes, displaced too. She was displaced in time. She was lost within her own mind."

To see it so clearly after the fact, and to have done nothing, said nothing at the time! To lose your own "personal narrative" is to lose your identity, the anchor and ballast on who you are in the world. No wonder Mum felt peculiar! And to think she gave me more than one opening, which I was too insecure and wrapped up in my own fears to take up. I understand it now and, as I do, as I let memory and feeling in, I can begin to imagine what this disease might mean as lived experience. Losing memory isn't like losing a cardboard box full of remembered things. It's not just the past that's lost but the present too. The whiteout that I'd imagined being splashed across Mum's brain was being splashed against her eyes, blinding her even as she could still see the mailboxes at the end of the lane, could still nominally read her old recipe for pastry. All these familiar things, these parts of her daily life had turned away from her, flipped over like pieces of a jigsaw puzzle the base of which is blank. And Mum experienced this, the turning, the blankness where once-familiar signposts staked the boundaries and laneways of her life. It's not like a Turing-test computer where information is correctly retrieved, or not, end of story. Here, there's the agony of looking, the embarrassment of getting it wrong, of not being in charge, the fearless roof walker in the eyes of your children, or yourself. No wonder Mum felt a tightness inside. And me? I still hadn't even considered that this had anything to do with me. I hadn't begun to let Mum's Alzheimer's into my life, unravelling the long-familiar patterns of how I saw her and related to her. I hadn't yet crossed the threshold into the zone of struggle and transmutation called mourning. I hadn't even found the door.

At the time, the door I had in mind was the door of some residence. Mum occupied a disease state that I wanted to leave to the professionals. I imagined that I would visit her in it from time to time, on my best behaviour, and that would be that. Meanwhile, I felt nothing; I was that aloof, and still withholding myself, though hiding it well behind being good and helpful: fixing the sewing machine when the threads got snarled up, making pastry and getting nutritious food down Mum's gullet, pumping good deeds into her shrinking existence.

At least with the diagnosis in hand, I could relax a bit. I had been vindicated in what I'd been saying to my siblings. The universe would unfold. Mum would go into a residence; it was only a matter of time. I even began seeing Mum's behaviour in a new, more generous light. She cared less and less about housework because she'd never cared for it in the first place. She cared less and less about conforming to the norm because she'd been eccentric all along. One of the unexpected items on her credit-card bill was five hundred dollars for a human-growth hormone touted as an elixir for memory and brain function. Turns out she'd seen an ad for this on one of the game shows she'd taken to watching on TV, and had phoned the 1-800 number they told people to call. Nothing strange in that nor in having bought an expensive, accessory-laden vacuum cleaner from a demonstration-salesman following up on a telemarketing pitch. If he was at all good looking and charming, no wonder! Mum flirted with the ambulance attendant when she broke her hip at eighty-five!

Good old Mum: Her world was getting smaller and smaller, that's all. She was simplifying, dropping what she couldn't handle, focusing on what was important, if only to her. From then on, I brought more and more of the food we had for our meals, and we cordially ignored the leftovers going sour and mouldy in the fridge. I routinely threw these out, and Mum didn't say a word. There was ease in the air between us, a new coziness too. Mum had begun to tuck her arm behind my elbow, lacing her fingers with mine when we walked to and from my car. Once she said, "You are a good soul." Another time: "You hold me in your heart." I didn't want to rock the boat. I didn't want dropping the boom to fall to me, and yet I'd moved Mum the last time. When it was time for Mum to move off the farm, it was I who kept the prospect in front of her, I who took her looking for a new place, I who helped finalize her choice on the Rideau River just outside

Kars—close to a colony of martin birds so that she could try starting a colony herself. I then got her to choose what furniture she'd move off the farm and arranged for it to be transported so that everything was ready for Mum coming back from Florida in the spring. As I look back on my procrastination, I think I didn't know my own strength. Still, I didn't want to push the river, only follow it, reading its course. As well, Miles and I had decided to separate, and Donald was three credits short of finishing high school and starting to apply to universities. I had enough on my plate at the moment.

One day I arrived to find the living room turned into a construction site: sawdust all over the carpet, saw, hammer, and various pots and cans of old rusty nails on the coffee table. Various lengths of lumber and lath were leaning against the sofa.

"Come see what I've done," Mum called out gaily as I carried the groceries into the kitchen area. I came over and followed the line of her finger pointing to a patchwork of lath and two-by-two she'd cut and nailed together to frame a set of shelves she planned on installing in the space between the top of her wardrobe and the ceiling. Unconventional, sure. But why not? I could see the pencil marks on the wood where she'd measured everything before she cut. I could see the split in the wood where she'd tried to use too big a nail at first. But I could also see that she'd correctly sawn wedges into the two pieces of wood that would hold the shelf inside the frame. So ingenious, so inventive. So Mum!

"What an engineer you are," I told her. She beamed, and kissed me exuberantly on the mouth.

I went back to the kitchen area to put the small roast I'd bought into the oven, and to clear off just the minimum of space I'd need on the counter to make an apple pie. The end was in sight; I could afford to even be nostalgic about the clutter. I looked up every so often to watch Mum at work, pencil tucked behind her ear, tip of her tongue sticking out as it always did with her, and me too, when concentrating hard on something, her finger going up to her face at regular intervals to push her glasses back up her nose, to whisk some loose hairs back into place behind a bobby pin.

A month or so later, the neighbour wandered over one day to tell me that Mum had forgotten to bring her beloved dog Coffee inside when she went to bed one night. This was late fall, the temperature dipping below freezing at night. He'd heard the dog whining when he was outside checking something before going to bed himself, and had quietly opened the back door and let her in. He looked at me hard after telling me this, as though to ask: What are you waiting for? I took to phoning Mum in the evening with a mental list of things to check off if I could. One morning Mum called me. She asked how I was. I said fine, how was she? She said fine, but there was a strange mist in the house. A mist?

I said I'd be right down, and she seemed glad, even reassured, which worried me even more, and made me glad that I was only a short drive away.

The house was full of smoke when I got there. She'd left the soup on the stove all night. It had boiled down to nothing, and started to burn. Mum was back in her bed, hoping perhaps to sleep off whatever it was that was wrong. I opened doors and windows, put on the kettle for tea, and encouraged Mum to get up, telling her that everything was okay. Then I sat her down on the sofa, took her hands in mine and said, "It's time, isn't it?" Yes, she said. Right then and there, I broached the subject of a seniors' residence, and she agreed. She also agreed to deputize me to find a place during the winter, when she'd go to stay with Janet at her

winter place in Arizona. Mum could move right in when she
came north again in the spring. That's fine, she said. Then I but-
tered the toast I'd made to go with the tea, and we sat there chatting about this and that.

"I'm ready to put my feet up," she said at one point. "Just
watch the world go by." She smiled at me. I smiled back. And it
was that easily accomplished. I kept the momentum going, using
emails to Jan as a way to relay choices for Mum to consider, first
River Park Place versus a second possible residence, then what
things of hers I might move in. Mum was compliant to the point
of indifference. Having finally let go, she was letting everything
go. I didn't spend a lot of time deciding among residences beyond
price, room with a view, and proximity to my home. I was looking backward, ensuring Mum could keep her dog and bring a
birdhouse to install on the grounds. I wasn't looking forward to
seeing how well they could support her as she continued to decline, beyond choosing a place with a locked unit for advanced
Alzheimer's and other dementias. But I avoided checking it out,
never got beyond the locked door at the entrance.

By the time Dick went to Arizona to fly north with her, I had
selected Mum's favourite chair, coffee table, pictures, knick-
knacks, plus the pendulum wall clock Mum had bought to cele-
brate Dad's retirement, and set them up in Mum's suite. I put
the duvet Doug and Norma had given my parents years ago,
which Mum had left unused, on the foot of the bed, and the
memory book, a scrapbook of photos and the anecdotes I'd
written to accompany them that I'd given Mum for her eightieth
birthday, on the coffee table. And, sure enough, when Mum
walked in, she seemed to feel she was home. Still, I brought a
foam mat and sleeping bag with me, thinking I might just spend
the night. And sure enough that's when it hit her, or when she let

her feelings out. I'd tucked her into bed, kissed her good night, watched her take her hearing aids out and her glasses off, and turned off the light beside her bed. Then I'd unrolled my bedding and prepared for bed. Suddenly, her light was back on.

"I'm to stay here then?"

"Yes," I said, walking over and sitting back down on the side of her bed.

"Till I die?" she asked me, and instantly I got it: all that time of denial.

"Yes, perhaps," I said, returning her look, as steadily as I could.

She kept looking at me searchingly. "This is where I'm to stay then?"

She wasn't denying, or avoiding the truth, just having trouble getting the sense of it to lie flat in her mind so she could understand and get a feeling for what this actually meant. I took her hand and nodded. "Yes, Mum."

She squeezed my hand, and nodded. "I'll try," she said.

I told her she had a feisty spirit. She didn't seem to register this. "I'll put it in my mind, then, and build from there." A pause. "I'll try my best," she said.

"Good for you," I said, and kissed her on the forehead. We said good night again, I turned out the light and lay down in my sleeping bag by the window.

Some time later, I heard a slight noise, and Mum was crouching beside me. "I've come over to consult," she announced. "First, is there an organization that runs this place?"

"Yes," I told her.

"Well," she said, "I'd like to talk to them about, oh, getting a pack of cards to play solitaire. That's something I can do myself." Then she nodded as though satisfied.

I watched her make her way back to bed, her pink-blossomed

flannel pyjama legs baggy around her scrawny ankles. I smiled at the sight of her tucking herself back into bed, taking her hearing aids out, laying her glasses down on the night table, turning off the light, lying down and pulling the covers up under her chin. I heard her sigh, sighed myself, then lay back down to sleep. But I couldn't get to sleep. I couldn't stop thinking of Mum stuck here playing solitaire. That this is how she saw it: all by herself here, me absent from the picture. And underneath, not surfacing yet except as a deeper ache of loneliness: the whispered thought that I'd helped to draw that picture. I'd helped deal the game, for us both.

3

The Clearance

The stillness of the place registered, but only in passing, mostly as an all clear. Mum was safely installed in the seniors' residence, having gone straight there after her winter in Arizona with Jan to find her single-room suite all decked out in what I'd guessed to be her favourite things. This left the cottage on the Rideau River empty of people but full of stuff, a clean-up chore that someone had to do it.

I took out the key from under the boot board, unlocked the door, and stepped briskly inside—the air like damp sheets on the line, the smell of stale breath. I kept moving. I crossed the living room to the window. Outside, the sun played shadow games with the clouds. I pulled back the curtains, and wrestled the window up. It was much warmer outside than in. I crossed the room again, opened the window in Mum's bedroom, then strode out to the sun porch and yanked on the damp-stiffened windows there. A gust of soft spring air wafted in. I stood there taking it in, almost scooping it up in my hands.

I opened the package of industrial-strength garbage bags I'd bought for the occasion, pulled one out, and flourished it full of air. Then I grabbed the sofa cover still sitting on an arm of the sofa. One of us, Mum or I, had managed to sew up the seam, but we hadn't put the cover back onto the sofa. And now, why bother? I pushed it into the dark gleaming space inside the bag, watched the plastic billow out as the cloth settled satisfyingly out of sight at the bottom. Next, I grabbed the ripped jeans, still pinned and waiting to be sewn, and rammed them into the bag too—pins and all. I kept walking, picking up things from hodge-podge piles on the coffee table, the end table, and even unused chairs: worn-out work gloves, a stained tea towel, old magazines, and copies of *The Watchtower* bought from some shy woman who regularly dropped by for tea and a small donation. Would she want to visit Mum at the residence? How could I find her?

I turned the corner into the galley kitchen, and saw the counter: the mounds of junk, the dust-caked layers of accumula-tion, all those lipstick-marked napkins, the clutter of empty jelly jars, the piles of seasonal to-do lists, thumbed with grease or dirt from the garden. How could I have stood it all that time? I grabbed and shoved: all the unmended broken things, the twisted twist ties, the useless bits of unravelled string, the restaurant sugar bags skidding off each other as I gathered them up. All Mum's time and energy wasted in all this hoarding, while she never had time for my son's birthday parties or awards day at school. I paused over the nozzle from the sprayer and the bolt from the lawnmower then pitched them in, and soon I wasn't thinking. This was a huge job and it had fallen to me to do it. Well, if I'd called on my older brother Doug, who also lived in Ottawa, he probably would have come. But he'd likely have tried to take charge. So I never called, and now here I was, with a couple of hours before I had to get home to make supper and help my son Donald with his homework. I'd make a good start at least.

I picked up a wad of Mum's parsimoniously saved and never re-used napkins, and used them to push everything to the edge of the counter and—*whoomp*! The whole lot of them disappeared into the capacious cavity of the garbage bag, a cloud of dust smelling of mouse piss, mould, and insect spray choked off on the rise. I secured the bag with a brand-new twist tie, and stood back, breathing hard. The counter looked huge, naked, and bereft.

I carried the garbage bags outside to the garage. Then, on a whim, I detoured to the garden shed and found Mum's gardening spade. It was a lovely spring day; maybe I could dig some of the weeds out of the garden. I hoisted the spade so I was holding it by the neck, like Mum always did in fact, the weight of the shovel nicely balanced. Then the sun came out from behind a cloud and caught the edge of the blade. I stopped, held it up to my face, and a rush of prickling heat went through me. My mother. This is my mother. I stared at the worn and dirt-covered spade. The sun had caught the cutting edge of the cast-iron blade, and I could see how clearly worn down it was, even chipped a little, from Mum's hard use of it, from her four-hour stints of gardening after she'd finished her main household chores of the day. She'd be out in the garden digging stones and old knotted roots out of a new bed she was preparing for her flowers. Who knows? Maybe venting some anger and frustration at her situation in life: four kids, a huge garden, and two households to run, only a few minutes a day to herself.

I looked at the blade, tears blurring my eyes, an ache I couldn't fathom deep in my chest. This part of Mum's life had passed away; she'd probably never use the spade again.

When my father died some twenty years earlier, I hadn't been there. My parents had gone to Florida where, with the sun and shark's cartilage, Mum was convinced she could nurse Dad back to health. He was dead within a week of getting there, news of it coming through a phone message left the next day with my husband, Miles. It was a Saturday, and I was out buying groceries. Miles met me at the door with the news: "Your father died last night."

The words went through me like I imagine a high-powered bullet passes through the body, making a neat, clean hole through the flesh and blood. It left a void, an absence so profound it was like my senses had been turned off. I couldn't hear right, I couldn't see straight, couldn't feel, especially after flying down to Florida that same day, and arriving to find no sign of my father—not even the stuff left over from his having been cared for, till the end, at home in his own bed and bedroom. There was nothing out of the ordinary. Mum had even packed away Dad's pyjamas and dressing gown. We sat together on the sofa in the living room, me on the end, silent, and Mum chatting about how kind the neighbours were being. Suddenly I saw him. Out of the corner of my eye, I saw my father, dressed in his faded old striped pyjamas, leaning against the doorframe of my parents' bedroom on the far side of the living room. It was just a flash, a momentary glimpse, but it was definitely Dad, collapsing in the doorway. And then he was gone. I sat staring at the spot hoping for more, the conversation continuing around me, the others oblivious to what seemingly I alone had seen. Many months later, prodding first Jan then Mum for the story, I came to some sense of what had happened. On the afternoon of the day before Dad died, they'd left him in the bedroom while they had tea in the living room. And he, afraid to be alone perhaps and yet with the cancer having cut off his voice, had dragged himself out of the bed and to the door. When he collapsed there, they rushed over and helped him back to bed. From that point on, Jan told me, one of them was always at his side.

I don't know why I saw my father's ghost that day. Perhaps it's because I was looking so desperately hard. Every fibre of my being was trying to find him, to tell him "I love you," to say good-bye. Perhaps my desperation helped to pull him out of the wood-work there in that spot where an imprint of his presence remained, a ghostly shadow of his own desperation a mere two days earlier. His energy might have seeped like blood into the warp and weft of the wood grain and my frantic energy might have sucked it out, brought it to life just for that flash of an instant.

It wasn't enough though. Not enough to comfort me, to hold me while I worked through my grief; only enough to snag me, sending my regular timeline into spasm, skewering me in that moment, impaling me in the woodwork. Some part of me got left there, while the rest of me carried on. I even caught an early plane back to Canada to keep a speaking engagement when most sensible people would have cancelled. I lived that split in some stupid errors in professional judgement I made in the fol-lowing months and years. I lived it personally too, as I let my marriage run into the ground, unable to speak my truth, to feel much of anything, except rage!

In her lovely novel *Memory Board*, Jane Rule chronicles the terri-ble unravelling, the radical unhinging that memory loss does to a person's mind, and how the caregiving main character moves to mitigate the damage with lists that marked all the minute passages of the day. Reading the book, I recognized this as an act of love that knew no boundaries. The imagination of one moved into the spaces vacated by the other, nosing out improvisations, totally unselfconscious, totally present, giving and unafraid.

I was envious of that intimacy because I didn't have it with my mother, and knew it; it was mostly a good performance, while the core of me remained aloof, and largely always had. From childhood, if I wasn't doing Mum's bidding or, in those brief moments when sickness made her vulnerable, taking care of her, I was running. At the farm, freed from chores in the afternoon, I regularly took off, usually in my bare feet. I practiced hurdle jumping over the winnowed hay in the lower pasture then slipped through the fence to feed the neighbour's horses. If I went in the other direction where the other neighbour kept cows, I followed the paths the meandering beasts made through the scrubby density of hawthorns, chokecherry and prickly pear, and emerged like an explorer into little clearings, my feet tingling from bits of rock and flayed twig. If I was lucky, I'd find a nice dried-out cow patty to stand on, warm under the sun. Some of my happiest memories from childhood are of me in one of those clearings, humming some Sunday school song and listening to the crickets, safely, happily alone.

Little had changed over the years. Building a career as a writer took me first to Edmonton then to Winnipeg, and I sent newsy letters home signed at the bottom "love Heather." The capital "L" word, to say nothing of the whole declarative statement "I love you," were conspicuously absent, even after work brought me back east to Ottawa and, after Dad's death, I moved Mum to within easy driving distance of my own family's home.

I gripped Mum's garden spade by the neck, squeezing the cool, unyielding metal. Mum was still here. *Is* still here, I thought, looking at the blade. Something raw and urgent travelled from my hand to my legs and feet. I carried the spade back to the house, and went inside. I turned around and went back out. I leaned the spade against the inside wall of the stoop, gave it a reassuring little pat then marched to the garage and picked up the first of the garbage bags I had filled. I carried it inside, undid the twist tie, and dumped the contents back onto the kitchen counter. A snort erupted from my nose and mouth, and I burst out laughing. Mum might have been revealed, laid out like an open book on the counter before, when it was still what her hands and inventive, hoarding mind had built layer by layer, item by salvaged item over the years. Now it was a mess of spilled garbage, with nothing to teach me anymore. Still, I felt better as I shoved everything back into the garbage bag, clearer in my mind. I had found the door, the way in to something I subsequently came to recognize as the state of mourning. I had found a way to focus.

For me, grieving a death begins well before the last breath; at least, it can. It begins at the point of contact, where and when you cross into the fullness of the experience, not just the circumstances of what's happening. Mourning commences when you begin to pay attention, starting perhaps with what blocks the way. For me, it was how Mum and I had related to each other, our dance of distance from each other: Me reaching out insatiably for her love and approval and her withholding it or doling it out sparingly, conditionally. Whatever its nature, our old relationship was dying as Mum was disappearing into dementia, taking who we had been, and how we had been together, with it. I had to grieve it, and contend with its blockages if I wanted to get to the other side, so I could follow Mum, even accompany Mum, on her journey into unknowing and, ultimately, unbeing. I wanted to be there, not half-heartedly, some part of me still holding back, afraid perhaps that Mum might still control me, overwhelm me. Nor did I want some perverse reversal of domination and appeasement, parent and child. I wanted us to truly come together so that, when the time came, I could gentle my skin against hers, could press my love against her inner ear as she went down into the darkness where death would take away her capacity to hear and feel my touch. I loved my mother enough that I wanted to do this, and wanted to confront whatever stood in my way, if I could.

Some instinct prompted me to return to Mum's cottage some days later with my camera, and I roamed the place like a tracking dog with a poor nose for scent, but sniffing still. I stopped in front of Mum's dresser, cluttered with all the little things she used every day: bobby pins, safety pins, straight pins, tubes of red lipstick. There were things she'd saved to mark a special occasion: a name tag from a reunion of the "girls" who'd served in the Red Cross during the war, another from a McGill alumni tea and fundraiser to which I'd taken her. There was dust over everything, and a fine network of long hairs dropped from when Mum had stood here brushing her hair vigorously every morning. I picked one up, then another, revealing a languid alphabet of dust-free lines where the hair had been. Here, an S, there an L and there an almost perfect O.

I reached for my manual Minolta slung over my shoulder, and took off the lens cap. The camera and all the actions involved in taking photos bought me some time, helped prop open the door to what I was doing. As an old friend Moira once observed, we ritualize the unknown as a way to face up to it, to wrestle it into revelation; my camera became my medium for doing this. Repeating the ritual motions—adjusting the shutter speed and focal length—slowed me down and allowed me to dwell in my

hands and eyes, opening my senses to the body of this remembered space. It brought me closer, helped me to be present to
what I'd spent so much time absenting myself from over the
years. I also used the camera to hone in, to find and focus in on
what I had particularly avoided. I'd learned to divine for water
when I was a kid at the farm, using a forked apple branch, and I
felt I was doing something similar here in this quest. The camera
was the stick while Mum's place and the tangle of the time we'd
spent here together was the ground, the currents of water were
my feelings running hidden beneath its surface.

I lifted the camera to my eye and scanned the top of Mum's
dresser. I adjusted the focus and held the camera attentively, as I'd
learned to hold the twin prongs of the still sap-rich apple bough,
attuned to its turning in my hand, living matter responding to
the life force in other matter. Nothing in particular caught my
eye amidst the clutter. I pulled open the top drawer, scanned the
neat roll of rolled up socks on one side, and an assortment of
underwear on the other. I pawed through the underwear, pulled
out an old padded bra stiff and rusted with age, then an old
garter belt. I held it up full length. It was so old the rubber nipple
had crumbled completely away on one of the straps. On another,
Mum had sewn an old shirt button to serve instead. How ingenious! I arranged the garter belt on top of some old cotton panties
in the socks and underwear drawer, and took a first picture. It
was a start, at least. I picked up the bobby pins, thinking I'd put
them away in Mum's bobby-pin box, and moved instinctively
toward the bathroom. Amazingly, the box was in the exact same
spot that it had been since I was a little girl. Despite all Mum's
moves, it was still on the middle shelf of the medicine cabinet in
the bathroom.

I hadn't bothered with the bobby-pin box when I moved

Mum's things into the seniors' residence; I hadn't cared. It was just an old E.B. Eddy matchbox after all; Mum likely wouldn't remember to miss it anyway. I held it now, the cardboard soft as old flannel, the sides sagging inward from years and years of use. I slid it carefully open, and there was Mum's hoard of bobby pins, the plastic tips long gone, the twin metal arms gaping or crossed over each other from Mum's habit of twisting them like that to make them serviceable again. Mum had two hairdos in my childhood memory of her. One was a bobby-pinned wave which she set into her hair with a double row of bobby pins drawn from a cluster bunched between her lips and pried open, one at a time, with her top front tooth. That was her daytime look, applied in the morning after she washed her face then dampened her hair with the facecloth. She kept the bobby pins in while she went about her day. Then with supper boiling up a storm on the stove primed for my father's return from work, she changed her clothes, took the bobby pins out of her hair, brushed it up soft around her face, and put on fresh lipstick. I often came into the bathroom to watch this final transformation, standing on the toilet seat cover so she could hand the bobby pins for me to put away in the cardboard box while she brushed out her hair and pinned it into a lovely, waved roll around her face. Then she took the box from my little hands and put it back on the shelf in the medicine cabinet, and picked up her tube of bright red lipstick. I watched as she applied a layer of this to her upper lip, and rolled the upper lip against her lower lip to spread it evenly. Then, smiling first at her finished reflection and next at me for being such a good and helpful little girl, she clicked the top onto the lipstick tube and put it back on the shelf beside the bobby pins, closed the mirrored door of the cabinet, and headed for the front door where, as if on cue, my father magically appeared and swept her into his arms.

Now I found a doily under a lamp in the living room, and set the bobby-pin box on it. I brought in the lamp and used it to light the scene. I focused, clicked the shutter, advanced the film, took a few more shots then stopped, my energy and enthusiasm gone. This was easy stuff, nostalgic Hallmark-moment stuff; I needed to go deeper, look harder.

So many books on grieving stay neatly, safely on the surface of things, saying "you're going to feel this, but that's okay" and "you're going to feel that, and that's okay too." Pat, pat, pat. Anne Brener's book *Mourning and Mitzvah* is refreshingly different. Grieving, she says, is a struggle. It's work. "Grief work" she calls it, and it takes time. Part of it involves the concept of *teshuva*. This is Hebrew for return or turning, she writes, although the word literally means simply "repentance." It is central to Judaism's understanding of death, and the confession plus forgiveness that this often requires—the necessary letting go.

I hadn't read this yet. I hadn't read anything about death and dying or even much about Alzheimer's either, just the blunt, bare-bones stuff in the pamphlets the doctors had given to us, defining Alzheimer's as "a progressive, degenerative disease that destroys vital brain cells." The language was so categorical and remotely authoritative, and I rather liked that at the time. Learning the difference between anomia and aphasia also took me through the motions of taking on Mum's situation, yet without getting personally involved. All those hard and fast terms did the knowing and understanding for me. They took me off the hook of dwelling on the lived realities of what Mum was going through, forestalled my taking the plunge into the fullness of what was happening, not just to Mum, but to me as well. I wasn't facing a thing at the time, only pretending, treading water as I learned some of the definitions, but not letting their meaning work me over, not letting the experience they referred to move me, drag me in. Phrases like "the presence of multiple cognitive deficits" were a wonderful shield. They were so coolly self-sufficient with no room for personal knowledge and interpretation. There was no role for me in possibly negotiating the extent and impact of those deficits, and that at first gave me comfort. Plus, they offered clear boundaries against which I could measure Mum's situation, placing her, objectively mind you, inside the category of disease, and leaving me out.

Now, as I came across the pamphlets tucked under some unfinished crossword puzzles in the nightstand beside Mum's old bed, they didn't interest me. I didn't have a clue about what I needed to learn, what I was trying to discover as I stumbled blind and ignorant through the rooms of Mum's old haunt. Yet I knew I was onto something, coming back again and again to Mum's empty house, wandering around with camera in hand, combing through the remains of my mother's old order, picking up things sticky with the resins of our old, fraught relationship, things that would tell me about myself.

I had the time too. Now that she was in the residence, Mum didn't need me anymore, not in obvious ways at least. Others made her meals now. Others cleaned her bathroom, washed her clothes, made sure she had a bath at least once a week. I popped in for tea or supper and, if I had time, I ran her a bath and washed her hair. Sometimes I came home to find phone messages like: "Heather, there's no meat in the house. Where do I go to get meat?" or "Where do I present myself when it's time for dinner? Do I just go out the door here?" In each case, it was usually a fairly simple matter of calling back. I also spoke to the manager. She arranged for the woman at the front desk to call and cue Mum if she didn't show up for a meal, and that took care of that.

Mum's dog, Coffee, however, was becoming a problem. More than once there was a suspicion of pee in the carpeted hallway, which management drew to my attention. Then someone reported seeing Mum digging a dog turd into the front flowerbed with her fingers. Word of that must have gotten around for the ladies at her table in the dining room didn't want Mum to touch them anymore. They didn't want to touch anything she had touched either. I tried paying someone in the kitchen, who liked dogs, to start taking Coffee out once or twice a day. But Mum was suspicious of this stranger at her door, afraid that someone would take her doggie away. By the time the management lowered the boom, the dog knew it was time too. When I visited, she'd try to bolt out the door with me as I was leaving. There was no obvious evidence of neglect. But often I arrived to find Coffee's water bowl dry and the lid on the toilet seat down— Mum felt it was unhygienic for the dog to drink from the toilet.

For weeks after I'd taken Coffee home with me, Mum left phone messages on my machine. Ingenious, devious ones too, including, one day: "They say I can have my dog back. So, Heath, if you know where my doggie is ..." Sometimes I laughed. Sometimes I felt a wave of sadness, largely sentimental, really. Mostly I just listened, shook my head, and pressed the delete button. I was still holding out on Mum, holding myself aloof from her in ways I was only now trying to discover, and resolve.

So what exactly was I looking for? What might I be holding against her? I remember the hand-me-down clothes, the size 16 school uniform when I actually took a size 10, and only being allowed to wash our hair once every two weeks. It was to save on hot water Mum always said, but the kids at school laughed and made fun of me as it got more lank with grease. The boys on the school bus scratched their combs against the back of the seats coming home, and I came running into the house crying, only to have Mum tell me to "stop snivelling." I shouldn't let the teasing bother me. I remember being given the role of Pitty-Sing in the Gilbert and Sullivan play, *The Mikado* at school, and Mum pulling an old sheet out of her rag bag, proposing to make a costume out of that. I was so mortified that I went along with a ruse concocted by a girl who had wanted the part, and traded my role for hers, playing the understudy. Then there were all the rules around the house—having to say "excuse me" if you burped, having to push your chair back in when leaving the table after a meal—any three infractions of which would cost you ice cream for dessert on Sunday. Of course too, there was the strap, and the stick Mum used to keep on a ledge under the stool in the kitchen for beating the dog. I hated that stick so much when I was growing up that I once dreamed I had burned it in the fireplace. I woke with a sense of the dream so strong I was weak with dread at what Mum would do to me for burning the stick. I never dreamed of the strap, but can remember it just as vividly: a brown leather belt, the buckle gone at the top, which Mum kept, rolled up tight, on the top shelf above the bread box in the kitchen. I don't think I ever got the strap, just spankings. But Doug got the strap, and I used to cringe because he would not cry, just hold it all in somehow, angry as can be. He was always being sent to his room for being what Mum called "bad," though often only for talking back to her, and he was always missing ice cream on Sunday.

On the sun porch, I pulled out the various tins and pots in which Mum had collected rusty old nails and screws and bolts. I dumped some out on the floor, remembering tedious hours as a child being sent outside with a hammer and a tin, my task being to hammer the bent nails straight again so Mum could use them making birdhouses and such. I took a few pictures, some with a depth of field to catch Mum's handwriting overlaying the brand name and logo: "Bolts" or "Nails," some with a shorter depth so only the bent and rust-encrusted old nails would be in focus. I kept going, groping like someone in a game waiting for word that I was getting warmer. I opened closets and cupboards, took the lid off things, letting my senses take it all in. I began to realize that it wasn't any one thing I was looking for, but the overall lay of the land, the weft and weave of how Mum and I had always related to each other: Mum always dominant, me alternately in hiding or suppressed, present only in the safe guise of performance.

Being the "dutiful daughter" had been my alibi, a mask of presence behind which I was essentially absent. And that wasn't good enough for what lay ahead. This much I knew, and it drove me like an untraceable itch as I prowled Mum's old home, uprooting things, holding my camera up to my eye. I was trying to find the pulse of resentment, of loneliness, whatever long buried feeling it was that bound me to the past, unresolved tensions still prickling like a wall of thorns between Mum and me. I took picture after picture—the fly swatters patched with wire and bicycle-patch glue, a pair of jeans with patches on top of patches, Mum's gardening spade outside. As I waited for something to pounce, I found myself just enjoying the images I was seeing, and Mum's personality shining through them, hard working, parsimonious, and creative. This was Mum, doing what she wanted to do, that's all.

I was back in Mum's bedroom, standing behind the door

facing the hooks and nails in the wall from which Mum always hung her work clothes to air at the end of the day. There were layers and layers of them stacked there from over the years. Now I noticed a tuft of faded red flannel. It was the dressing gown my father had bought Mum for their first Christmas together, before he was sent overseas in the war. She'd worn it all through the days of my childhood, its creamy chenille ribbing on bright red flannel belted tightly over her pyjamas as she first made Dad's tea, toast, and porridge for breakfast, and sent him off to work on the 7:45 train, then got us children up and, as we were old enough, sent us off to school with our bagged school lunches in hand. All this came back to me as I stood looking at the dressing gown. The red of the gown's main fabric had faded, and I could see where Mum had sewn a patch along one of the cuffs, and stitched red thread to close where a seam had simply worn away at the back of the shoulder. I noticed all this, but mostly with a detached interest. For something else had snagged my attention, was drawing me in. Something about the way the dressing gown hung in the shadow behind the door. Something about it drew me back to when I was still too young to go to school but before Dick was born. Mum and I had a game we'd play in this quiet time after everyone had gone and we had the house to ourselves. While Mum was putting her tea things onto the tray, I'd scoot upstairs ahead of her for a game of hide-and-seek. This day I opened the door to the closet tucked under the eves in their bedroom. Correction. It must have been her afternoon tea, when she'd sit on the bed for a second bit of quiet time before everyone got home. Because in the morning, she'd still have had her dressing gown on. This day I snuck into the cramped dark space under the eaves where Mum kept Dad's and her clothes. The dressing gown was hanging from a nail in the shadow to the right of the door. Leaving the door open a little, so I wouldn't be scared in the dark, I scrambled into the space behind the dressing gown, pulling its soft chenille and flannel in around me. I heard Mum come upstairs, and went absolutely still. I heard her set down the tea tray, and I went even more still, holding my breath, poised for her singsong voice calling my name, her smile, and her hands reaching out to gather me into a hug. Silence. Total quiet. Darkness and silence. Nothing. And then, some motion nearby, hangers being moved. I stirred, and suddenly, "Oh, there you are!" Mum pulled the dressing gown aside and beamed down on me. "What a good girl you are," she said as she helped me up, straightened my clothes, and ushered me blinking out into the light. She'd finished her tea already, and was changing into her good clothes to be ready for supper with my father. She'd forgotten all about me and our game. And I'd been such a good little girl for not making a fuss while she sat oblivious and had her tea.

I got a lamp from the other room, and positioned it to accent the shadow behind the bedroom door. I moved the door, back and forth, back and forth, until I settled on leaving it open just a crack. I was aware of my breath coming thick and harsh, like a diver coming up for air as I peered through the viewfinder, focusing in. I felt the shutter make its decisive click, and thought, pay attention. I advanced the film, and moved in for another shot. Mum had drunk her tea and read her book that day while I had huddled there waiting and waiting for her to come. I must have felt at least a little lonely and forgotten, maybe scared too.

I moved the lamp closer, lighting the details of Mum's old and by-now-filthy dressing gown: the chenille worn down to nothing at the hips and across her belly where it sagged. I breathed in deeply. I stepped back to focus into the space between the folds of the gown, at the exact border where the frayed tuft of the chenille gave on to the shadow where I would have crouched. I adjusted the aperture, the shutter speed, advanced the film, and *click*. And again, *click*. Once more. Memory surfaced and I was in its thrall: my sense of being forgotten, yes. Mum's rushing us past the moment, and my accommodation. Good girl, good girl for not whining or complaining, for not saying a word. I lowered the camera and wiped my eyes. Ah, dear little girl scrunched down there in the darkness, knowing at some level that Mummy wasn't coming; she'd forgotten all about you. Yet, here's her dressing gown, its smell familiar, soothing you, taking you into sleep, while Mummy read her book and drank her tea. So like myself, a busy woman with to-do lists of my own and a son who seemingly understands my need for what he once called my "quiet time," in a poem he wrote for me as a Christmas present when he was fifteen.

This grieving work I had stumbled into wasn't just "letting go" of all that I'd held against Mum. I also had to let myself go, past performance, past waiting for Mum to find me, approve of and affirm me. In the grieving, "we have the opportunity to strip away parts of our self-image that aren't authentically our own," Brener writes. "As we do this, we begin to reclaim our lives." Or claim it for the very first time, I wrote in the margin, with an exclamation mark. I remembered how Mum used to introduce me as "one of those women's libbers," and how resentful I felt. Yet I used to talk about this part of my life to Mum with such smug superiority, reminding her of how important the work of my life was (compared to hers): not just the paid work of teaching at the university, speaking at conferences and writing books, but my feminist activism on abortion rights, and women and technology. In 1981, I was one of the women associated with the "Ad-hoc committee of women and the constitution" that organized a renegade version of an official conference, which the federal government of the day had cancelled. Thirteen hundred women answered the call, put out through informal telephone networks, came to Ottawa, and filled the Railway Committee Room in the West Block of Parliament Hill to pass resolutions that resulted in the equality clause being included in the Charter of Rights and Freedoms. It was an important historical moment, and I was at pains to communicate how important this was to my "stay-at-home" mother. Still, I could have shared with her some of the wicked, wild moments too: my favourite is from one late Friday night when the Commons custodians lent us carts to transport the conference kits from Centre Block to West Block through the tunnel connecting them. As the carts gathered speed on the downward slope, we jumped on the back of them hooting and hollering, wild women having a blast! If I'd told Mum that, re-living the sheer adventure of it all, it might have kindled some solidarity between us, brought us closer together. But I didn't.

I wandered into the kitchen to put on the kettle, taking on the thought that maybe I was the problem, not Mum. The Hebrew word for grieving, *teshuva*, does first and foremost mean "repentance." And it occurred to me that Mum never came to Donald's school events because at heart I didn't want her there. Perhaps I didn't even invite her, just assumed she wouldn't come anyway, when really I wanted my son to myself: on stage for being on the principal's honour roll, on stage for winning the school art prize, once again. My dear, darling Donald, my perfect child, who snuggled into my arms long after he'd stopped breast-feeding, who found me when he got home from school every day and clambered into my lap as I sat back at my desk, having saved whatever writing I was working on when I heard the door open, and turned off the computer. Evenings, friends told me later, I'd leave women's organizing meetings early in order to read Donald a bedtime story if it was my week, not Miles's, to put Donald to bed. Summers, we went on mini hikes to the local parks and beaches and, when he was older, bicycle rides along out-of-the way roads in the countryside, sometimes dropping by Mum's place on the Rideau on the way home.

I was the perfect parent. I might have even dangled that in front of Mum. Certainly I never let her get too close to him—this child named after her beloved husband and who, with his sweet, quiet nature, strongly resembled him as well. When Doug's boys were in their teens, he arranged for each of them in turn to spend a week at Mum's cottage on the Rideau, so Mum could teach them manners. But I did not. I came close one year. We arrived with Donald's bag all packed. But first Mum wanted me to stay for lunch; she'd made pancakes as a special treat for the occasion. But the pancakes were flat and hard and soaked in roasting-pan grease, and the maple syrup had gone mouldy from sitting too long on her shelf. Donald turned to me, tears in his eyes, saying he didn't want to stay, and so we left.

I took my mug of tea and sat with it between my hands in the living room, letting my gaze float unfocused in the steam, thinking of Donald and how he'd changed in recent months. He'd had to switch schools to enrol in a semestered program so he could finish his last three grade thirteen credits by Christmas, but he seemed okay with that. He had been accepted by one university already, and had been invited for a "portfiolio inter-view" at the Ontario College of Art, where his art teacher was sure he would be accepted. But lately he'd become withdrawn, would stay in bed with the covers pulled up over his head some-times. And even if he made it to school in the morning, he'd leave class; just up and walk out. Where was he now, I wondered, and was he smoking dope, which I was sure he'd been doing more and more of late.

I took my tea, and wandered over to the small bookcase where Mum stored the few books she'd brought with her in the move off the farm: mostly bird books, one about gardening, the Bible she'd been given at Trafalgar School for Girls, and a linen-bound book of poetry called *Magic Casements*. As a child, I used to hurry home from school, hoping to find Mum still having her tea upstairs on the bed. If I was quick, grabbing the green plastic drinking glass from the upstairs bathroom, and this book of poems, I might prolong that precious time. She approved of memorization, and so I'd get her to choose a poem that I could work on, snuggled in beside her on the bed. Once, I managed to learn an entire poem of twenty-some lines: "When Day Is Done." The day's still-to-be-done chores, the state of supper preparations, Mum's battles with predator birds, starlings and sparrows, all were blissfully forgotten for the moment.

I put the tea mug down, got up and went into Mum's bedroom, bent over and looked under the bed where, all along, I knew Mum always kept them: the dry-cleaner bags she'd saved since the days of sending Dad's business suits to the cleaners. She used them to kill the predator starlings she caught in her trap birdhouses as she fought to protect her beloved tree swallows and martins in the birdhouses she had built just for them!

Mum constructed her lovely birdhouses with hinged lids so that she could clean them out in the fall and put in fresh bedding. She also constructed some with a frame around the hole, across which a trap door could slide when pulled by a string. I grew up hating the sight of those strings, pale, white snake-like things strung across the lawn and leading to the window behind which Mum concealed herself, curtains and drapes cleverly drawn.

Sometimes the siege went on for days, and we tiptoed around the house as Mum got more and more worked up on behalf of her swallows, more and more furious at the starling with its long pointed beak that could peck out the swallows' eyes, or break their freshly laid eggs. Sometimes Mum waited, hovering, for hours, willing the starling to go into the trap house so she could pull the string, and kill it. Sometimes she ended up with a migraine, she got so angry and upset. And so I thought one day I would help her, because it meant so very much to her to get rid of these awful birds. Mum and Dad were out somewhere and a starling was hovering around the trap house. I peered through the gap in the curtains, and there it was, sitting on the perch. What if it went in? Mum would be so pleased with me if I caught it. Even if I only tried. I picked up the string and went into Mum's squinting, watching pose, keeping very, very still. Then it did go in, and I pulled the string. And it didn't come out.

Now what? I'd leave it there; Mum and Dad would be home soon. But they weren't. When I looked out the window, I could see the birdhouse moving; clearly the bird was jumping around in there, trying to get out. I'd better bring the birdhouse in. And so I did. But the bird wouldn't settle down. If anything, it was now making even more fuss and commotion, banging its wings against the wood, tossing bits of straw and twig around inside. You'd think it would get tired eventually, but it didn't. It wouldn't give up. Maybe I should put it out of its misery. That's the phrase Mum always used. It's important to put it out of its misery, quickly, she always said, as if this was the point. Putting it out of its misery sounded like an act of mercy. And so I got out the dry-cleaning bag Mum always had at the ready. And now, all these years later, I took myself through the motions with the idea of capturing the bag-enshrouded birdhouse on film. I flicked the sheer plastic until it bulged open wide, taking in air that set it wafting light and gently around the box of Mum's old trap house. It was so easy to draw it over the top, to tuck the ends in underneath. The stubby bit of wire sticking from the back end of the trap door was so easy to see through the plastic, easy too to grasp and pull backward in the event of a bird having been trapped inside so that it could fly out into the seeming freedom of the clear plastic, and be killed.

I lit the scene carefully. I took up my camera, looked through the viewfinder, and took a deep breath. I took my time, focussing carefully on the shifting, elusive plastic that kept drifting, billowing slightly with the air currents from the window. I could feel the fear, being drawn into Mum's sphere, her callous ability to kill. *Click.* To take decisive action and not feel a thing. *Click* again. I prepared another shot, focusing now on the bit of old wire protruding sideways from the light length of slim board that served as the trap door. I would have pulled a piece of wire like this one that day. *Click.* Next, I focused on the hole itself, bleeding into darkness at the edges, swallowed by darkness in the middle.

In the darkroom later, I positioned this negative in the frame, adjusted the focus and set the exposure time. I turned off the fluorescent light, and sank into the soft red-felt glow of the darkroom light. I pulled a sheet of blank white photographic paper out of the drawer and set it in place. I flicked on the timer, and watched the light etch its shadowy story onto the page below. Timer off, I took the paper and submerged it in the developing bath. Patches of darkness began to appear, coalesced into shape, sharpened into focus. I stared into the open hole of the birdhouse, the plastic floating like a veil around the edges. Tears came to my eyes. I picked up the tongs and transferred the photo to the stop bath. I felt a prickling in the palm of my hand. I'd done it that day. I'd done it exactly as I'd seen Mum do it, though I thought I'd always turned away, made sure I wasn't in the room. I grasped the wire and opened the door, and the bird flew out of that open hole, straight into the wall of plastic. And though my mouth flew open at the time, my hand did not. My hand resolutely did what I'd seen Mum's hands do so fast and efficiently. I grabbed the flapping bird and pulled the plastic sheeting in close around it, cutting off its flight, cutting off its breath. But it didn't want to stop breathing. It didn't want to stop flying. It struggled in my hand. My little-girl's hand that wasn't very big, wasn't very strong. The bird kept struggling and struggling against the skin of my palm while I held on, willing it to stop.

I stepped to the overhead light switch and flicked it on, tears streaming down my face. The photo was perfect. Keenly in focus. Sharp and true. I held my open hand in front of me. The prickling gone, but the memory of it lingered. It had been there all along, all these years since: the memory of the bird's struggle for life, of my killing it, my complicity in this thing my mother did. Sure enough, Mum had been so pleased, so proud of me when she got home and found the starling, still wrapped up tight in the dry-cleaning bag and the bundle duly jammed into the toe of the rubber boot Mum kept handy for precisely this purpose, just in case the bird wasn't quite dead yet, and struggled enough to let some air in and even get free.

I pulled the print out of the wash tub and grabbed a clothes peg to hang it up to dry then stood looking at it hanging there, and it came to me: I never did this again. I never trapped or killed a bird after that day. I had figured out how to be true to myself, and quietly stuck to it. The picture blurred as the tears poured out of me. Just quietly poured. It's a good thing I had the darkroom to myself that afternoon. I developed more pictures, and I cried some more, and then I unpinned the clothes pegs and gathered up the prints: Mum's things, my memories.

I sorted through the stack of photographs, choosing a selection to show Mum next time I went for a visit. Not the shrouded birdhouse shot. We were past being able to discuss that now, and there was no need. Mum had run her life her way, I was running my life my way. She made her choices, I mine. Still, part of me was still hooked into looking for Mum's approval because I felt deflated when she showed no real interest in the portraiture I'd made of all her hoarded things. The one exception was the E.B. Eddy matchbox of bobby pins, the crumbling wreck of the cardboard set off nicely by the doily.

"Ah, you found them," she said, and immediately wanted me to bring the bobby-pin box back to her. It was Nov. 11, 2002, and perhaps because it was Remembrance Day, I had decided I'd stay for dinner. I cleared up the tea things while Mum changed into her Black Watch suit, put on her high-heel shoes, then brushed her hair and put on her lipstick. Then we walked arm in arm to the main dining room and to her appointed table for the later, second serving. Mum's was a corner table by the south window, her seat beside Mrs. Margaret Taylor who sat with her back to the wall, the better to see all the comings and goings in the dining room and who, by now, graciously suffered me to call her Margaret. We took our seats and the serving staff immediately came to pour Mum a cup of tea. I put my napkin across my lap and listened as the other women talked about the cenotaph ceremony they'd watched on the news. Suddenly Margaret reached out toward my mother's arm. Too late; Mum scooped the contents of a margarine container into her tea, the margarine packets being kept in the same bowl on the table as the creams and milks. I watched horrified as Margaret signalled for one of the serving staff. "I usually watch her," she said in an aside to me, whether apologizing or reassuring I couldn't tell. Clearly, Mum had been slipping, and I hadn't been around enough, or focused enough, to notice. Mum hung onto her teacup as the young woman reached for the saucer. "No; it's alright," she said. "I'll just drink it." She was clearly flustered, didn't like a fuss being made, didn't want to waste good tea.

One of the women had been a nurse during the war, and talked about that as the table settled back down to eat.

"Mum was in the war too," I said when she'd finished her story. "In London, with the Red Cross, weren't you Mum?" I turned to her, sort of handing the conversation off to her, and normally she'd run with it because some of Mum's happiest memories were from when she played angel of mercy to wounded soldiers in hospital during the Blitz. Mum looked at me, smiling.

I smiled back. "Remember when you were in London?" I asked, smiling and nodding, giving her a verbal nudge.

Mum looked around, taking in her table companions all smiling at her expectantly. "Oh yes," she began. "The gang was all there." She looked at me. I nodded and smiled encouragement back. "And we went along there." She paused, looking at me again. "Didn't we?"

She frowned slightly. "You were there, weren't you?"

I looked down to hide my tears, my utter devastation. Then I reached out and took her hand. I even smiled. "That was another time, I think."

"Oh," she said, and smiled back, reassured somehow, and then we ate, leaving the talking to the other women, including Margaret Taylor whose mind was still so intact that she could remember the First World War breaking out. She was a child at the time, and staying at a family cottage on some remote Ontario lake. Her Uncle Archie came rowing across the lake that morning fairly shouting the news across the misty water: War had been declared. And then he was off. Off for the big adventure. He never came back.

4

Learning to Talk All Over Again

When we finished supper that evening, Mum couldn't eat the Remembrance Day cake she'd chosen on top of her usual ice cream for dessert, and so we carried it back to her suite. Once there, I left her standing in the middle of the room holding the cake while I plugged in the kettle for tea. I was learning to let her be while she sorted things out on her own, no longer needing to look after, to prove myself, to cover up.

"I might just keep it for later," she said, indicating the cake plate in her hand. "I'll just put it . . ." She paused, and I looked at her briefly before bending to get the tea canister out of the cupboard. "You know, where I keep them."

"Yes, over there," I said, gesturing toward the little bar fridge beside the bathroom. Mum filled it up with various bits of leftover meat, uneaten cake and other stuff she carried away from the dining room folded up in a napkin or on a side plate. She then forgot all about them, and the staff regularly cleaned things out. I never asked her why she did this, nor asked the staff, who never mentioned it to me either. Perhaps it was paranoia, or simply the need to be in control of her food again.

"Oh yes, of course," she said, and set the cake down on top of the fridge. Then she walked back across the small room, sat up on the bed, and watched me. I can't remember when I'd taken over getting the tea things ready. But I was conscious now of my hands going through all the motions her hands had normally performed: warming the tea pot, getting the cups and saucers out of the cupboard, finding the milk pitcher, and pouring milk into it. The complications of even this sequence were beyond her now, though not the pouring of the tea.

I took the cup that she handed me, and we settled in side by side on her bed, the fingers of my right hand comfortably laced with the fingers of her left one. I told her about my day, she nodded and said, "oh yes" and "that's nice," and then we lapsed into silence, listening to her wall clock chime seven o'clock.

Mum held her cup up in front of her. "Such a lovely cup," she said, as she'd said every time over tea for the past several months.

"Yes," I said, "it's a beautiful cup." We sat there admiring its vivid motifs and colours: the ripe purple of a painted plum, the perfect blush on a peach and a pear, and the radiance of gold inside the cup itself. It was Mum's favourite teacup, given to her by "Buntie," her oldest girlfriend from school, who in turn called Mum "Beaver." (The joke of it was they both shared the given name of Anne.)

The teacup I used was a gift from Buntie's mother, Mrs. Thom, whom Mum continued to visit when I was a child. It had a more subdued yet classically graceful design in pale green and gold. I rarely saw these or any other of Mum's "good" teacups when I was young. They were stored on the tippy-top shelf in the kitchen cupboard. But I caught a glimpse of them when I was standing on a chair getting something else, and often wished them down. And so, when I moved Mum's stuff into the seniors' residence, I made a point of moving these particular cups and saucers too. Now we used them every visit, just these two, the most beautiful and, perhaps the most precious, though by now the names Buntie and Mrs. Thom were long forgotten.

I always waited for Mum to draw attention to my cup after we'd finished admiring hers. "Yours is lovely too," she said.

"Yes, lovely," I said, turning to smile at her. Whereupon, Mum turned to me, lips puckered, for a kiss. And I kissed her, a good solid kiss on the mouth, the way she liked it.

Tea on her bed, with those same teacups and the same appreciative comments about them every time, became our regular ritual, and every time it seemed to take on more lustre, more resonance almost, like a melody line in a concerto for the piano and violin, offset in infinite variations by first the one and then the other instrument. It resembled too the gestures of approach, retreat, lingering, and longing in a lovers' pas de deux. And increasingly I could just enjoy them for what they were, gestures of our connection. I could dwell in these moments sharing a cup of tea with Mum, and be satisfied.

Mum was extending herself less and less in activities and outings and even in conversation. It left me with less and less to talk about, less and less to do. Still, I made the most of watering the plants that Doug regularly brought on his visits. I cleaned the birdcage, added water and fresh seed for the two budgies that my brother Dick in Montreal had brought when Mum could no longer keep her dog. But then even the birds got to be too much for Mum. Often, she opened the cage to check on their feed, to speak to them, who knows? And they escaped. She called me desperate, and I'd have to get the staff to intervene. Looking for Mum's pearl earrings at least was getting easier. If she'd hidden them, they were usually in the back of a drawer in her bureau. Sometimes, she'd merely dropped them, or knocked them onto the floor and either not noticed or forgotten all about them.

Every so often, I brought the memory book from the coffee

table, and we turned its familiar pages, following the chronology of Mum's full and active life. Sometimes it triggered some memory: an anecdote from the house where she grew up in Sherbrooke, when we came to that page, or the picture of her most loyal childhood companion, a cocker spaniel.

"Brownie," Mum said, her voice tapping a vein of pure joy at seeing an old friend.

I didn't task her with questions, didn't try to draw her out. When she lost interest, we sat there drinking our tea in companionable silence, listening to the birds, the chime of the clock, our breathing comfortably in sync. Periodically, Mum squeezed my hand, and I squeezed back; it was conversation enough.

I remember when my son Donald was growing up, learning to make his way into the world, and to articulate his observations. I noted each step forward with pleasure, marvelling as he learned to apply newly acquired words to the things he saw. Once we were holidaying in Prince Edward Island and passed a lighthouse. "A blinking home," he said. I smiled at this sweet evidence of his stumbling toward an adult naming of the world, and I avidly recorded it in my journal. Now I was witnessing these steps in reverse, a journey not into knowing but away from it, into unknowing. Mum's sense of language was going backward. At first the syntax and general ordering of words into coherent sentences gave way. Now the words and intelligence behind them were disappearing. They were being disappeared. It was a perversion of ellipsis, not the compression of intelligence but an implosion, a falling in on itself, the original meaning of sentences and sentence sequences in tatters. Trying to imagine it, I think of Mum on a beach. Alzheimer's was eroding more and more of what had been distinctive footprints and sandcastles complete with little banners of identification, leaving Mum stranded, making her own strange sense in the sand. I could almost sense the waves at work, dissolving Mum's remembered life, and my part in it too; the tide dragging everything off the beach and forever away. And yet, not quite everything. If I kept walking with her, taking in everything as it happened, I could tell that something was being left on the beach. A familiar stranger was taking over more and more of the person I had grown up knowing as my mother. If I stayed in touch, not looking for the old Mum, but opening myself instead to the new, using the touch of her skin in my hand, the look in her eye, her frowns, her sighs and smiles as my guide, I could know her still. I could know her by giving up my own familiar ways of knowing, and opening myself to unknowing too.

It wasn't easy. In a journal entry from shortly after the Remembrance Day incident, I wrote: "Woke up last night grieving for Mum, and all the things that have slipped away from her grasp. She can hardly talk anymore—beyond simple statements like 'it's so nice here,' single words like 'lovely.' Abstractions seem to be gone. And if she embarks on a longer sentence, she often gets lost. 'It used to be that, uh, when things were like that.' Yes, I'll say as though she's made a point, and she looks relieved, lapsing into the safety of a smile."

I now know that this way of talking, including Mum's tale of London during the war that Remembrance Day supper, is typical of someone with dementia, whether stroke related or from Alzheimer's. Empty words and sentence fragments signify difficulties in "lexical access." In fact, the words and the thinking person knowing what she wants to say might still be very much in there, just blocked and perhaps only in that instant and on a bad day. I only learned this later, when reading an account of some-one actually experiencing Alzheimer's in psychologist Steven Sabat's *The Experience of Alzheimer's Disease: Life Through a Tangled Veil*. "It sort of creeps in," this man, Dr. B, told Dr. Sabat, in his attempt to explain how, if he just relaxes and takes his time, the word he's looking for will sometimes come back to him. I only fully grasped what this meant, in terms of continuing to know and honour the person living with dementia when, years after Mum's death, I saw the play *I'm Still Here,* every line of which is drawn from interviews with people living with Alzheimer's. The one I most vividly remember was when the dementia-afflicted mother says to the caregiving daughter: "In my heart I felt you knew that I was still here."

I choked trying to stifle the sob that line evoked because I hadn't known as such that Mum was still there. But I wanted it to be true. In fact, for a while I simply took that position, stubbornly insisting that it was, because I'd been arguing with my brother Doug about this very point for years. Doug took the view that when memory goes, the self goes too. Mum was gone, he insisted, replaced by a frail old woman grateful for love and attention. Well, I could acknowledge that she'd changed alright. But I argued that the essence of Mum, the core of her vibrant if wilful self, was still there every time I walked in the door to her suite. Still, what little medical literature I'd read by this point, pamphlets at the memory disorder clinic and the doctor's office with their point-form crispness and relentless list of negative symptoms seemed to support Doug's view. They bristled with words like "degenerative," "multiple deficits," the "shrinking brain," the "death of the mind." I stopped reading any further, because I didn't want Doug to be right. Possibly too, there was my own guilty conscience, at how I'd availed myself of the science to move Mum into a residence, have her committed in a sense.

Three years after Mum's death, I sought out Dr. Linda Garcia, an expert on communication breakdown in dementia. I'd already learned how central language is to identity, from philosopher Ludwig Wittgenstein's notions of how we create the world we inhabit through words to social psychologist George Herbert Mead's classic thesis, outlined in *Mind, Self and Society*, that the mind and the self are "social emergents," with the "vocal gestures" of language serving as the "mechanism" for this emergence. Is there still a self, I asked Dr. Garcia, when the capacity to make, to parse, and to follow these vocal gestures goes? Is there still an intact person trying to relate despite the empty words, the crippling disintegration of language? Long after it was too late to make any difference, I still wanted an authoritative answer to my questions.

By way of saying yes, that someone is definitely still there, trying to communicate from within the rubble of Alzheimer's, Dr. Garcia took me through the basic building blocks of language and communication: from phonetics, which is the ability to simply produce sounds, to phonology, which involves forming those sounds into intelligible words, according to learned rules. Next, there's syntax and grammar, through which we organize words into sentences, then discourse, which involves linking sentences coherently, and, finally, conversational discourse, through which we use language to communicate intention, to explore and exchange meaning. It's an intricate cognitive tower involving semantic memory—the storehouse of remembered concepts, and episodic memory—remembered names, words and events, plus executive functions, through all of which we organize thoughts and hold the thread of conversation in our minds. With dementia, the tower becomes a Tower of Babel filled with senseless babble as the neuro-plaques associated with the disease cripple the ability to pull up the words we want to say, to stay focused on and follow a conversation, and even to name things correctly.

I recounted an incident from when I'd taken Mum back to her old cottage in Kars for the weekend. As we drove past a billboard saying "Clean Fill Wanted," she undertook to read it. "Clear water fall," she said. Oh, I answered, appalled at this evidence of how her reality was completely divorcing itself from mine. In fact, Dr. Garcia suggested, Mum started off okay, but then some combination of short-term memory loss and the loss of the mental gymnastics necessary to correct herself—plus perhaps Mum's pride and bravado—took her elsewhere. It's a breakdown in "pragmatics," she said: the mind's ability to self-correct speech through self-monitoring, a casualty of short-term memory loss. As well, what Edwin Shuttleworth and Steven Huber (in "The Naming Disorder of Dementia of the Alzheimer's Type" in the journal *Brain and Language*) call the "referential boundaries of words," are eroded. The differences between words begin to blur with the result that a related word will surface on the tongue rather than the right one.

During that visit to the cottage, I was gathering up stuff to take with me and Mum out in the canoe. Suddenly Mum said: "Now, you're Janet."

She was looking at me hard, and frowning. "No," I said gently. "I'm Heather."

"That's right," she said, and nodded as though patting this correction firmly into her brain. "You're Janet." I fumbled getting the life jackets and the paddles into the boat, feeling as though I had been forgotten. As a character in Michael Ignatieff's novel *Scar Tissue* says, "If she failed to recognize you, you ceased to exist." I was jealous too, thinking that clearly Mum loved my sister more than me. I didn't realize that with the feedback loop broken, Mum was incapable of noticing her own mistake, of even recognizing the gap that had opened up between her sense of reality and her diction. Words were increasingly just that, free-floating sounds, signposts detached from the pathways of know-ing, perhaps with just a vestige of familiarity as they floated away. Out on the water, Mum tested herself on something else. She held up the paddle, and said: "saddle." She looked at me. "No," I said. "Paddle." Mum frowned, nodded and tried again: "Saddle." I nodded as though she'd got it right, and carried on.

I ran this story past Dr. Garcia. "Same problem," she said. "A breakdown in pragmatics."

"Yet it's devastating," she said, "because we define who we are through words. Any person who loses the capacity to com-municate, especially in our modern industrial society versus the bush where identity is tied more to physical capacity, it starts eat-ing away at your identity and who you have defined yourself to be. It's a real grieving process: How can I define myself anew?"

But language is inherently social, with two people making sense through words together, or not. Public thinking about physical handicaps has shifted focus from the "crippled" person in isolation to how the environment itself handicaps people in ways that can at least be mitigated through ramps on curbs and approaches to buildings. Similarly here, Dr. Garcia told me. Oth-ers can help someone with dementia make sense, through what a colleague of hers calls "conversational ramps." I've now dis-covered a rich, and growing literature addressing the social con-text of dementia, including a plethora of "communication enhancement" aids such as memory-book-like photo scrapbooks, memory-cuing lists of daily things to be done, and sticky-note reminders. They also suggest using short sentences conveying one thought only, avoiding metaphoric language that might be taken literally; avoiding open-ended questions like "what do you want to do?" in favour of ones requiring only yes or no answers. There's also the less-cluttered time and space that people with dementia need to survive, and simple things like asking, "do you understand?" And, always, the literature says, take your time, listen, encourage, go with the flow. Don't correct facts and botched memories. Forget phrases like "remember when?" The past is gone. Only the present remains; let that be enough.

Looking back, I did okay figuring a lot of things out for myself: using the memory book as a prompt, making a chart of Mum's daily schedule with times when she should go to the dining room on the main floor for breakfast, lunch, and dinner. Another list with everyone's phone number on it was taped to the wall by the phone.

Still, I sometimes felt that I was shrinking, like Alice in her adventures through the looking glass, because Mum's world was getting so small. It was claustrophobic. This is why families are also part of Dr. Garcia's focus, and why the Alzheimer's Society has support groups for caregivers too. For the person with dementia, "it doesn't matter if conversation breaks down; they're beyond that now," she told me. "But it's devastating for the family. It affects your identity too." She looked me at me steadily, as though she knew about Mum mixing up my name with Janet's, as if this sort of wounding happens all the time, the pain of it gagged into silence.

"You have to start redefining what communication is," she continued. If you can. She confessed that her mother has dementia, and recently its advance has blocked her ability to follow what Linda is trying to say long distance on the phone. "It's cut off my lifeline, which is the phone," she said. I thought of Janet far away in Edmonton and what she must have felt.

I got lucky, being the one who was there week in and week out, though initially I'd felt almost the opposite: Definitely unlucky at having been left holding the bag, so to speak, stuck with caring for Mum in her decline as the daughter who lived the closest. Now, I wouldn't have had it any other way, and the tricks or gimmicks for helping Mum were only the start of what I learned. I tapped into a whole new way of communicating with my mother, and opening myself up was integral to it.

We're used to communication being like a phone line, clear signals moving efficiently along a neat linear line. But Mum's sentences no longer strode boldly one after another across space and time, sure of the point they were making. They still started boldly enough, with words like "There was a man. . . ." or "And then we went to . . . ," but then they veered off, petered out, dwindled away. Week in, week out, the sentences got shorter and slacker, more and more riddled with lapses and gaps, subsiding into silence. I learned to hold my tongue and not second guess, nor even to deflect Mum to another subject. I learned to breathe, just sit there and breathe. I learned to go slack too, sinking into the silences, ready to move on, or not to as well. At any given moment, this was where we might be: mid-sentence somewhere, and meanwhile, here was Mum's hand in mine, her face searching mine for a response of some kind. Sometimes she shrugged. "Ah well," she said, and I smiled and shrugged too, letting it go as well. I learned to accept, make myself at home in this new realm of communication that was strewn with broken sentences, with "empty phrases," and increasingly laced with silence. This was our visit time now, the new texture of our connection. I learned to take my cues from whatever was available, though this had less and less to do with the cognitive stuff of normal communication. Our "conversation" became simply what was left as the grammar, sentence structure, and finally even the words fell away. We were still two people communicating with each other, with intent and meaning flowing back and forth.

Mum's crumbling capability with words, matched perhaps by my crumbling expectations, was also a medium of transmutation, bringing both of us into a new way of relating to each other. An old way too, in the sense that we were tapping in to the primal root of what human communication is all about: the bedrock rhythms of expression and connection, as the common root word for "communication," "communion," and "community," meaning "to share with" suggests. In his book *Musicophilia: Tales of Music and the Brain*, Dr. Oliver Sacks recaps the long debate on whether music or language evolved first in human culture. On the one side, he cites Charles Darwin and his hypothesis that "musical tones and rhythms" were used by our "half-human ancestors," and that speech arose "secondarily." Contrariwise, he cites Herbert Spencer for whom music arose from the "cadences of emotional speech." To me, however, the similarities are more important, between the embodied cadences of speech and the lyrical speech of music. Or rather, as I moved close enough to partake at least a little in Mum's un-learning curve, the differences fell away, leaving us with "prosody," the rhythmic aspects of speech that bind two people in a matrix of pure communing verbally and with gesture. Rhythm is the essence of relating, its immaterial glue and grammar.

Canadian linguist and poet Robert Bringhurst does a lovely job of excavating this aspect of communication from the ancient Greek classics. In *The Tree of Meaning,* he dwells on a line by Alkinoos to Odysseus, which in English reads as: "You tell a story with a minstrel's skill." Bringhurst then digs deeper, explaining that the Greek phrase used for telling a story actually translates as "tell your way across" a story, because the key verb used, *morphazo* means "to make a sign, to gesture."

Unwittingly too, I was learning to accept and adapt myself to Mum's shifting sense of time.

Phrases like "take your time" and "be in the present" are worthless advice to someone who is chronically busy and over-committed, as I tended to be at the time. How do you go from striding boldly from one task to the next, traversing a clear, linear progression of time to the seeming nothingness of simply being, alive in the present moment with someone who's losing all their anchors to the world and its story lines? It took the medium of what I was actually doing to slow me down. I think back to when I started taking photos of my mother's old house as I was cleaning it out, how I took my time then and, equally, let time take me as perhaps my first step. Similarly, the ritual motions of preparing our tea slowed me down enough to ready me for the increasingly halting conversations on Mum's bed in her residence. Over time, these in turn went to work on me, massaging me into quietude, the hovering, perpetual now.

Mum's capacity to "tell" time, to comprehend and work with conventional clock time had pretty well gone by the time the geriatric neurologist got Mum to draw a picture of an analog clock with all the numbers positioned in a circle and the big and little hands in place, and Mum failed the test miserably. It signalled too that she was leaving the world run by clocks—linear time—behind. I had to step away from it as well if I was to succeed in staying in touch with her in ways that mattered. I had to reacquaint myself with time embedded in the medium of life itself: a baby nursing, a flower unfolding, tea leaves steeping in the pot, an ocean's waves creeping up and down the beach with the tide.

I didn't do it instantly, easily, or gracefully. There were days when I ran screaming from the residence, wanting to do things, accomplish things, or at least to have a decent conversation that went somewhere! But gradually, I found that I no longer fretted about what Mum was trying to articulate, no longer caught myself thinking, what a useless waste of time. Increasingly, especially when immersed in the rituals of tea, I could stay with Mum's reality, and go along with her sense of time as ebbing and flowing, breathing in and breathing out, meditative.

Linear time didn't die as such. Its thread just sagged, got snagged, and stalled as her conversation sagged, snagged, and stalled. I grew used to this, to dropping away from purpose and direction, to sitting in the pause, listening attentively, patiently waiting for whatever Mum said next, and quietly ready for that to be nothing at all, maybe squeezing Mum's hand and feeling her squeeze back. Gradually, I got better at simply drifting into the pool of Mum's gathering silence, in sync with my breathing, matching it to Mum's till I was floating, in something companionable, and rich with the sounds and sights of now all around us: the birds in their cage, the pendulum clock ticking back and forth on the wall, our shoulders warm against each other on the bed. As clock time broke down more and more, I forgot to be anxious at its disappearance. I even participated in that disappearance by not prompting, not asking questions.

The staff now came to run Mum's bath and supervise her getting into it. But she refused to let them help her bathe. So often I assisted her, washing her hair, now thin and almost entirely white, but still long and worn up in a roll across the top of her head. On her birthday that year, she sat in the bath I'd run for her after dinner in the dining room. I'd put in apple-blossom-scented bubble bath, and Mum was delighted. She patted the piles of gleaming bubbles, and softly began to sing: "Happy birthday to me, happy birthday to me . . ." It bothered me to see Mum like this, like a child really, playing with the bouncy bubbles. So I poured myself a scotch from the bottle Doug had brought for visitors, and sat on the toilet seat watching her. Eventually, I even hummed along. She looked up and laughed, her nut-brown hazel eyes brilliant in her rosy bath-warmed face. I can see them still.

After the bath, I usually laid out fresh underwear for the morning and, while she put her pyjamas on, I looked through her clothes in the closet, tossing what had food stains or smelled a little into the laundry bag, then cased her little suite sniffing for a pair of urine-soaked pyjama bottoms or pants that she might have taken off and shoved out of sight behind the little fridge or bureau. More recently, my search sometimes turned up an adult diaper, which they were making her wear now at night. Mum hated them. She sometimes took them off in the middle of the night, and hid them somewhere—though not always before she'd peed in them.

I usually did this bit of housekeeping while Mum finished up in the bathroom so that, when she emerged, pink-cheeked, powdered, and pyjamaed, we could sit together quietly and, if it wasn't too late, have one last cup of tea.

We always had tea, and always side by side on her bed. If it was afternoon, we looked out the window at the river and the large park in front of it, the geese stalking the lawn, the squirrels chasing each other through the trees. I talked about my day. Mum said "Oh?" and "that's nice." Increasingly too, I told her not just about my work day, which was easy, but also about my son Donald who wasn't well emotionally or perhaps even mentally, though the doctors hadn't yet offered a clear diagnosis. In the past, she would almost immediately take charge, telling me what to do. Now she just said, "That's too bad," and squeezed my hand.

Eventually I took over pouring the tea, not just making it. Mum's arms were simply too frail to lift the teapot, her grip too weak to grasp the handle. Plus, the paraphernalia on the tray were no longer familiar enough to cue her actions; instead, they just made her anxious and confused.

I still brought her dog, Coffee, on my visits, though Mum soon forgot that the she had ever been her pet. Coffee became just an animal that she called "doggie" and patted for a while. Eventually, she forgot the dog was in the room at all, and Coffee started lying on my side of the bed during our visits. Other residents still recognized her, though, and it was often a slow walk down the hall as an old gentleman reached a tissue-paper-like hand to pat Coffee's head, or a shrivelled arthritic old lady bent down from her walker to say "Hello, Coffee dog." I felt a ripping up inside me, particularly when someone called Coffee by name. By some stroke of luck, these people could still remember not only their own world, but Mum's as well, while Mum herself could not.

Still, it felt good to just be there with Mum in her room, to settle into our tea ritual. She sat on her side of the bed and I on mine, next to the wall. "Another?" I asked, just as she had always done over the years, and I poured her a second and third cup. "Thank you," she always said when I handed it to her, that round of our ritual complete.

Teacups in our laps, shoulders warm against each other, Mum and I sat. Invariably, eventually, she remarked on how lovely her cup was, and I agreed, and then she allowed that my cup was lovely too, and again I agreed.

Time flowed in and out with our breathing, like the ebb and flow of the tide, "tide" being the Old English name for time. In those days, time wasn't just called tide; its meaning for the largely rural people of the day was implicit in the nature of tidal action: that is, the rhythms and cyclical flow of life itself. That's essentially what time meant before modernity and the invention of clocked time and, with it, new meanings of time associated with, for example, the eight-hour day and being "on time." While sun dials and even water clocks marked time's passage, its premodern meaning was still vested in physical and bodily actions, one moment breathing into the next, one action, one gesture into the next. That's how Mum and I related to each other now, communicating with each other through reciprocal gestures and touch, and the repetition of ritual phrases. We were in our own little zone, an ebbing and flowing now.

One day, Mum pulled her hand out from its nesting place holding mine, and held it up. Now that she had stopped grubbing in her garden or doing much of anything with her hands, her nails had grown long. I asked Mum if she'd like me to cut them. Yes, she said, and immediately sat up straighter, holding her hand out ready for me to do it right away. I got the clippers, and fumbled around for a while trying to get the angle right, realizing too that the only other person whose nails I'd cut were my son Donald's when he was just a boy. How easily his body had slipped into place next to mine, not so long removed from my breast when he was a baby, and my lap when he was a toddler. Now here I was learning to fit my mother's angular body next to mine. It felt awkward and wrong at first, her bones jutting out. But over time, slipping in next to Mum, towelling her hair, helping her step into clothes, became as easy and unselfconscious as it had been with my son. Cutting Mum's nails became just one of many things I did for her as Alzheimer's made its inexorable advance, erasing every means she'd always had for expressing her existence in this world, from complex conversations to simple words for things, and even the doing of things themselves.

Doing Mum's nails became a ritual of grieving too. She'd told me once, indicating her hands, "They're useful hands. They don't hesitate to get things done." Now her hands were limp and white, not just with longer nails marking her retirement from digging in the garden, repairing birdhouses, scrubbing potatoes for supper. The cuticles around the nails and the skin between her fingers were cleaner than they ever had been in the past. They used to be stained with dirt, the cell lines in her skin not just engrained but steeped in the material existence of her life. It had taken months, almost a year, for her hands to change, to become what they were now as I held them while cutting her nails: pure white and unsullied, almost bloodless. It made me want to plunge my own hands into the dirt, to find some deep and tenacious root that I could grasp and wrestle with, dark juices staining my fingers. Yet I continued sitting there, holding Mum's flaccid fingers in mine. And as I held them, so soft and clean, I mourned for the hands that had disappeared without a trace. Hands that had held the strap, yes, had held my head roughly, getting me to "hold still," while she cut my hair once again too short and in a style that made the kids at school laugh at me. Hands too that had picked beans and all the other vegetables that fed me, and had frozen them for suppers through the winter. Hands that pounded rusty nails straight enough to hammer them into salvaged bits of board to make birdhouses or shelving. And now they lay still, waiting on my own hands, as busy in my life as hers had been. As I clipped Mum's nails now, I could feel her breath on my neck, and greedily breathed it in.

Some months later, I persuaded Mum to reply to a late Christmas card that had been rerouted from her old winter home in Florida. It was from Val Horne who, along with her sister Phid, had been friends from her childhood in the Eastern Townships of Quebec. Since the note had conveyed the sad news that the girls' brother had just died, I thought it would be nice if Mum could write a short note acknowledging this and maybe sending her condolences. I suggested some phrases Mum could start with then watched as her hand pushed the pen carefully into the curvature of cursive letters. I'd always been struck at the spidery quality of old people's writing, and here I was watching the pattern being enacted. Partly it was how much Mum had lost strength in her hands. Partly it was her faltering memory played out on the page. Mum had always written in a bold, quick way in everything from her to-do lists to the letters she sometimes composed and sent off to the prime minister or the president of some large corporation telling them how to run the country, or their business. She never wrote to anyone more junior than that, and always used her good fountain pen.

Now, penning a simple, short note of condolence, she stumbled in the upward sweep of a "T." She lost her way part way through a word, or even a letter, and stopped mid-stroke. I sat beside her trying to recognize what letter or word she was trying to get out, trying to simplify the message. Eventually, Mum got out the words: "Too bad about Sam," and we stopped. And then Mum amazed me. She watched as I tucked the card into an envelope and addressed it then said: "He was the most peculiar of them all." I looked at her. She nodded, raised an eyebrow and smiled. "But then he was the son, so he was allowed to be."

Well! Had I helped draw that out of her? And if so, how? By urging her on to this task even though I realized early on that it was beyond her? Or simply by sitting there on the bed beside her, my breath warm and mingling with hers over the page? The scientific literature talks about how physical cuing can help draw out a word that otherwise would be considered "forgotten." It also talks about how enabling communication involves an "enabling social context." I think back now to that splintered, spider's web writing, what a tip of an iceberg it was, the fecund realm of feeling and thought still teeming inside, surfacing into some feeble scratchings on a page, but there nonetheless, still there!

But the scratchings were getting fewer and fainter, and there came a day when even Mum's memory from childhood was gone. Looking through the memory book had become my way of tracking this. One day we flipped to the page with Brownie, her dog-friend from childhood. Nothing; no recognition. Another, the last day we sat looking at the book together, we got to the page with a lovely photo of Mum carrying a bucket of water along the thin pier her father had constructed at the family cabin on a remote lake in Quebec.

"Who's that?" Mum asked.

"That?" I asked, pointing to be sure.

"Yes," she said.

"That's you," I said, though I could barely get the words out, I was so stricken by the question, Mum's seeming separation from her self.

"Oh?" Mum said, as if she couldn't believe, or make sense of, what I'd said.

I probably smiled and squeezed her hand. She probably

smiled and squeezed my hand in return. I put the book aside, and the moment passed.

I woke up that night with tears aching to be shed, another piece of the Earth cracked and gone. I had to grieve it, every disappearance, every mark of Mum's decline, and usually did so in the middle of the night. Sometimes I got up and wrote in my journal. Sometimes I just lit a candle, and let the feelings surface. I think of it now as integral to my own journey of unknowing, not just following Mum on her journey (into unknowing), but accompanying her, at her side. It's as though I had to live and feel each one of these losses, these blanking outs, these accumulating "deficits" in Mum's cognitive capacity, feel them as though they were falling away from me too. It mitigated the sense that Mum was moving away, because to a certain extent I was moving with her. It was almost as though we were moving together, the elements of what Mum could no longer say and do were like bits of clothing dropped on the floor, or landmarks glimpsed outside a train window then gone.

As I cut Mum's fingernails, helped her into and out of pants, blouses, and pyjamas, I also learned, or remembered from mothering Donald as a baby, how much communication is rooted in the body, and the more basic senses of touch, of gesture, of eye contact, perhaps even of breath. The minutia of this became a medium—not just for expressing and communicating love and, here, grief, but a medium in the sense of the nutrient culture in a petri dish enabling what's been inoculated there to grow; a medium of emotional, almost spiritual, intimacy. I didn't imagine that its tissue might help convey me, even tenderly, into the territory of death and dying, but I think it did. I knew only that this simple bodily contact kept me grounded and, as it did, helped convey Mum and me into a whole new realm of talking.

Now, though, it was the sound of the words and their tactile sense that I savoured. They meant more to me now than the semantics, the specifics of what was being said.

I don't know when I developed the habit of accompanying Mum when she went to the bathroom. It was a way to watch for bruises if she'd fallen or for anything else there was to take in. One day I noticed she had no panties on. Oh, she said when I pointed this out, and shrugged not wanting to bother with them then.

"They'll keep you warm," I told her, and quickly fetched a pair of her favourite, flannel panties from the dresser drawer. She sat there on the toilet totally passive, totally patient, as I took off her pants then put first one socked foot and the other through the leg holes of the panties. Her legs were inches from my face, the skin white and scaly, small blotches here and there where she'd banged herself on something and there'd been some bleeding beneath the skin—standard procedure with someone on anti-stroke medication. I pulled the pant legs back over her feet then, taking her hands, pulled her "upsy-daisy" to her feet, feeling the resonance with, but equally the dramatic differences from, Donald's childhood, when I pulled his perfect baby's body up on the changing table, and hugged him close.

Now he was out there in the city somewhere with an illness of which three doctors had finalized a diagnosis: a chronic condition of his brain bio-chemistry requiring ongoing treatment. I'd also signed the papers formalizing a separation from my husband. By comparison, coming to visit Mum was easy. Easy refuge too.

Helen the residence's social convener left a message saying

that Mum had seemed "lost" to her that day. She didn't specify whether this was inward or outward, for Mum was often getting off the elevator on the wrong floor and would wander around trying doors until some staff member, or another resident, brought her back to her room on the second floor. Thankfully she no longer ventured outside on her own as she had when she first moved in and regularly gotten lost. The management had a chain bracelet made for her, with her name on it, plus the address and phone number of the residence. Mum railed about it at first then grew used to it on her wrist. By the time the traffic lights at the busy corner down the street stopped being anything more than blinking orbs of yellow, red, and green, and the street itself disconnected from her sense of who and where she was, Mum had stopped going outside on her own. In fact, she was increasingly reluctant to go out at all.

I'd noticed that Mum was getting more and more confused. With my number prominently atop the list of phone numbers I'd taped to the wall, she still phoned me periodically. But when she got the answering machine, she often didn't know enough to just speak her message, and I'd get a voice saying, "She's not there" or just some frustrated breathing and a hang-up. What messages she did leave named more and more things she wanted me to explain. Lately too, she said she wanted to go home, though home for her was no longer the cottage on the Rideau River, nor the farm nor Florida. It was Sherbrooke, where she imagined her father still lived.

Once I called Mum on the phone. After several rings, she picked it up, but she didn't say anything when I said hello. Then, from a muffled distance, as though Mum had the mouthpiece to her ear, I heard an exasperated mutter: "They just want to know that you're there," and she hung up. I knew that the front desk staff had to phone Mum again and again to get her down to the dining room for meals. I knew that they were getting fed up with this. Perhaps the feeling was mutual.

Another day I arrived and found Mum standing in front of the mirror in her bathroom, a clutch of black bobby pins sticking out of her mouth, her hands holding a clump of her hair high over her head. She was on the brink of twirling her hair around her fingers before fixing the roll of hair against her head with pins. It was a style she'd always worn and it suited her well. Now though, she was clearly stuck. Even her hands were losing their memory. They were lost, disconnected from her brain, frozen in mid-air in front of the mirror. Mum seemed to be frozen too, the bobby pins sprouting from her pursed lips, the look on her face verging on panic.

"Can I help?" I asked, stepping in beside her. I reached for her hair, and she relinquished it. Then I rolled it up and made a game of pulling the bobby pins, one by one, out of Mum's mouth. The amazing thing was how much my hands had learned over the years from watching Mum. When I was finished, I held the collapsing cardboard E.B. Eddy matchbox while Mum put the leftover bobby pins into it. Then I placed it on its customary middle shelf in the medicine cabinet. And then we had tea.

Still, Helen's calls were gentle cues, and when the director of care called me in and said it was time for Mum to be moved to the locked "assisted living" floor, I knew that it was. They had two rooms available on this floor with its simplified layout and more extensive level of care. They wanted me to take a look, and I quietly followed the woman for a tour. She was surprised when I said I wanted Mum to make the final choice, but okay. I think she was surprised too when Mum chose the room neither of us had favoured. It had a setback space by the west window and chickadees in the spruce tree just outside. She wanted her bed set here, she said, though it was far from the pull cord to call the nursing staff if she needed help for anything. It didn't take long to move Mum's few things and treasures to the new room downstairs. She settled in there quickly, and we continued our familiar routines.

5

Medical Power of Attorney

Part of me wanted to stay where I was, snuggled in the clasp of Mum's hand in mine, just the two of us in our own little bubble of time. Part of me, though, was alert. I knew Mum's world had shrunk, and that her capacity to do what little she still could do derived in part from being on this floor, behind a locked door, what the literature calls "sheltered freedom." The "lock" involved said it all. It wasn't some sinister, remote inscrutable affair, but a keypad mounted low enough on the wall that anyone could reach it, with a code consisting of 987* that never changed. It was laughably simple, for me. Yet for Mum, her custodians might just as well have left an old-fashioned length of chiselled metal casually in full view on the table beside the door, locks and the keys to open them were that far beyond Mum's reach to grasp and make the connections. It was up to me, to us—her four children—to negotiate the larger world and its formal codes and keys.

The law is very clear, I've subsequently learned. If a person is deemed incompetent to grasp the implications of choices that affect their life and health, someone else must decide for them. If a family isn't willing or able to take this on, the state will intervene with all its cumbersome procedures for evaluating a person's capacity not only to understand and communicate but also to reason and deliberate. This is crucial. Making medical treatment decisions requires enough "cognitive capacity" to both comprehend a proposed action and to judge how it relates to one's goals and values and what "the good" in life actually means, and to communicate this to health professionals. This two-part capacity is called "competence" and is deemed a "threshold" distinction under the law. If there's any doubt, a formal evaluation determines whether you have it or not. If not, that's it: someone else must decide for you.

The point of a living will, or medical power of attorney, is not actually to take over people's agency as much as it is to extend its intent on their behalf when they've crossed that crucial threshold and are no longer considered fit to articulate their intent for themselves. The living "will" aspect establishes what the person's general will is and what values inform this, and names a substitute decision maker. To have maximum effect, though, it is accompanied by an "advance-care directive," which lends the force of declaration to the vaguer indication of values and priorities. It's a harrowing responsibility to take on once a person has slipped below what could generally be considered the threshold of competence, because it usually involves withholding certain medical interventions, and this can hasten death. It's a power that can be ill used; elder abuse has become a legal category on its own. No matter what, it's treacherous territory, not just legally and ethically, but personally.

I'd blown it the first time round myself. This was in 1995, when Mum came down with pneumonia. She was on the verge of driving down to Florida, as she'd continued to do every fall long after Dad died. Usually, Doug's wife Norma drove down with her, and Janet flew from Edmonton to share the driving back in the spring. Mum had packed most of the many things she took with her into the car, and had wrapped the packages of frozen beans from her garden in newspaper, tied them tight with binder twine and stored them back in the deep freeze until the moment of her departure. The next morning, following her annual routine, she'd wedge them into cardboard boxes in the trunk of her car, and zoom off, insisting that the beans would stay frozen during the two and a half days driving south into the Florida sun, though in fact they didn't. Mum was normally wired and excited at this point. Yet I found her strangely listless when I arrived for a goodbye afternoon cup of tea. When she had no appetite for the cinnamon bun she normally indulged in, I got out the thermometer. Her temperature was high enough that I said something when Doug and Norma came by to fetch her later. Whether or not I actually said "pneumonia," that's the word that paced the back of my mind. They too were concerned, enough so to take Mum to see her doctor, who urged her to stay. But Mum insisted that she was perfectly fine, and so Norma got in the car, and they set off. Almost immediately, Mum was too tired to drive. As they drove the highway bypass around Philadelphia, Norma wanted to abort the trip, drive to the airport, and send Mum back home by plane. But Mum said, "Certainly not!" She just needed the warmth and sunshine of her place in Florida. Still, she ate almost nothing, hardly even touched her tea, and increasingly, she sagged against the passenger door and dozed. Norma phoned Doug, who promised to contact Dick. Meanwhile, Norma kept driving south, while Mum slept more and more, still not eating and hardly drinking any tea. When they arrived at Mum's winter home, Mum went straight to bed, leaving Norma to unpack and put everything away. Now what? Norma was booked to fly home the next day, but she couldn't leave Mum like this. She might die. Then the phone rang. Dick happened to be in Florida, taking care of his mother-in-law who was also ill. He was at the airport, about to board his own flight home, and had thought of calling Mum's Florida number to say hi just in case Mum had gotten to Florida herself; he wasn't even aware that Doug had been trying to reach him.

Norma answered the call and immediately told him: "Your mother is *not* well." Dick came straight away, and immediately had Mum hospitalized. Being a respirologist, he could read the situation. He could also read the doctors who took charge of the case. Incompetent, he thought, and arranged for a medevac plane, coordinated its arrival in Ottawa with Doug, who called me with background and the hospital room number. I arrived to find Mum flat on her back, surrounded by machines and festooned with plastic piping, feeding oxygen into her nose and intravenous nourishment plus heavy antibiotics into her arm. She was also in isolation for fear that what she had was more deadly and contagious than simple pneumonia. So, like everyone else who entered, I enveloped myself in one of the pale yellow gowns provided, donned a face mask and put blue fabric slippers over my shoes. I peered at Doug similarly gowned and masked, and we both peered down at Mum. We whispered, as did our feet, moving through a fog of strangeness, fear, and not knowing.

Mum pulled through. The isolation order was lifted, and the intravenous was replaced by trays of hospital food. Doug visited Mum regularly, often sitting beside her bed at mealtimes, lifting spoonfulls of mush toward her lips. Once I arrived to find him getting Mum to sign a document. Turns out, this was to give legal power of attorney to my sister Janet and my sister-in-law Norma. I was shocked at this, and miffed at being excluded and left in the dark. It had to be done, and right away, Doug told me. Moreover, he added, a medical power of attorney should be put in place too, though he left that hanging.

He had arranged for Mum to come home with him to convalesce. But for some reason, Mum chose to come home with me instead. I never spoke to Doug about this, never even stopped to wonder why. I was just grateful to be back in the loop. She was weaker than any of us had realized, and needed another blood transfusion to boost her hemoglobin. Still, she steadily gained strength after a week or so at my place and, as she did, I began to think that maybe I could take charge of the medical power of attorney myself.

Some of it was sibling rivalry, admittedly. But I was also influenced by my father's death. I'd felt so excluded, only learning about it in a phone message the day after he'd died. According to arrangements Mum and Dad had made with a Florida funeral home on their own years earlier, there was no viewing at the funeral parlour. No funeral either. Dad would be cremated without ceremony, without anybody present. So there was nothing to focus on; nothing to serve as a touchstone, a lightning rod to ground the mad grief I felt at the time. I can remember a lot of stiff meals, some outbursts of laughter that got more and more hysterical as we all got into it, but no tears. We all took our cues from Mum; nobody broke down or otherwise made a fuss. Then we dispersed, each one back to our own lives. I was almost catatonic, for months, totally void inside, cut off from everything! I started drinking heavily, trying to jump-start my feelings I think.

No matter what, I didn't want a repetition of that time. I didn't want to be excluded, didn't want documents to once again leave me out in the cold. So I seized the moment of having Mum to myself to do some research on what a "medical power of attorney" or "living will" entailed. I wish I'd phoned Doug for his legal help. But I was afraid he'd want only Dick as a surrogate decision maker. With Dick as the doctor in the family, and Doug as the lawyer drawing up the deed, I didn't see much place for myself, nor have much faith that they would grant me any. Yet I was the person who was most involved day to day with Mum, at least that's how it seemed to me. So I sought my own advice, and proceeded on my own. I typed something that looked legalese enough to me in the printout. I ran it past Mum, who vaguely agreed, though was largely uninterested, and waited till Dick came from Montreal for a visit after Christmas. Once he was settled on my sofa beside Mum in what she'd established as her favourite spot, I showed him the document I had drawn up. It didn't say much in fact. Being a writer, I'd pumped up the rhetoric, striving for something formal and slightly arcane. There were phrases like "in accordance with my strong convictions and beliefs, the directions and wishes here expressed are to be carried out. . . ." There were no statements from Mum's own lips indicating her values or her will. Only a line to the effect that in the event that "there is no reasonable expectation of my recovery . . . I be allowed to die and not kept alive by medications, artificial support or heroic measures." Pretty pathetic as I re-read it now. But for me, the important thing was to have something, something that also named both Dick and me as Mum's substitute decision makers, acting in consultation with my older sister and brother of course.

Dick looked at what I'd written only briefly, gave me a brusque nod of assent then we had Mum sign it. He then tossed it onto the sofa and took my proffered cup of tea. Whether he said anything to Mum, or she to him, I don't know. But by the spring when Jan flew down to Florida to drive back north with Mum, my "medical power of attorney" had been ripped up. Janet had also either volunteered or been deputized to "speak to Heather about it." I remember the moment: as I heard myself being spoken to, my face went so stiff it felt like I'd been slapped. I was so ashamed. I'd acted prematurely. I had made a mistake—in the fullness of all my insecurities as who I was at the time, and where I stood in our family's pecking order.

Now, with Mum in her mid-eighties and clearly on the decline, taking action felt right. I was confident, even calm. I began by seeding the idea of a "medical power of attorney" in a phone conversation with Dick, recapping the care director's assessment of Mum when they'd moved her to the secure wing of the residence. I told him a few of the things that I'd noticed happening lately, keeping it clinical because that's what he tended to hear best, and that way he'd likely take me seriously. I also spoke to Jan and Doug, proposing that I could have an initial conversation with Dick, and maybe prepare something for them to comment on. Jan seemed happy enough to leave it to us; happy at a division of labour that left her dealing with Mum's finances, paying the bills at the seniors' residence, while Dick took care of health matters along with me in the day to day. I can't remember what Doug said. Perhaps we didn't actually talk, just exchanged phone messages or emails. I then proposed to Dick that we find some time to talk. I'd spoken to my friend Janice MacLean who'd drawn up a "health-care directive" for her own mother when she was in a long-term care facility, opening up the middle ground between "Do not resuscitate" (do everything short of the most heroic measures) or "palliative" care (do virtually nothing). I told Dick that I could get a copy of this, plus the forms the seniors' residence had, and bring them to the farm next time I came for a visit.

I instinctively chose the farm because it was our spiritual home as a family. It had been bequeathed to Dick in my parents' joint will, and after Mum had moved to the small cottage at Kars near Ottawa, he took it over as his family's weekend retreat. Over the years, with help from his wife Robyn and two daughters, he'd upgraded the bathroom and windows; he'd repainted the walls, kept up the fencing, the sugar bush and barns, as well as Mum's flower and vegetable gardens. He also added a veranda facing the "back forty" where the stands of pine and spruce we'd planted as a family grew tall and darkly lush, home to deer that ventured out into the pasture at sunset, and where everyone now gathered for a cocktail at the end of the day.

Having come for the whole weekend, I could wait for the right moment to surface. It came early Sunday morning. Neither Robyn nor the girls were up yet. So we could easily slip away, coffee mugs in hand. I think it was at that point that I asked, "To the rock?" Dick nodded and led the way. Originally, just a large pink granite boulder hauled to the side of the field in the early stone-clearing days, it had taken on the stature of a "family" rock over the years. It was flanked by the pasture on one side and, on the other, shadowed and overhung by the first stand of spruce and pine trees we'd planted as a family. The soil of the farm had become leeched and eroded after the place had been abandoned in the postwar period, and the worst was here on the upslope from the river that formed the front border of the farm. And so our family, including skinny, sickly seven-year-old me, had begun tree planting in this spot, with Dick joining in when he was old enough to hold a sapling. Years later, I was doing research at the Ontario archives and decided to track down what I could on the two hundred acres of land that my parents had bought. I wrote it up as a story, and gave it to my father one year for his birthday. Turns out, the farm had originally been part of a clergy reserve then, once it was available for sale and development, had passed through several hands as the original owner sold it over and over again, taking back a mortgage then foreclosing when the hapless landholder was unable to make the annual payments. Finally, however, a man called Duncan MacMillan established a farm and family on this place, clearing the land, pulling stumps from the field, picking rocks, and generally wrestling the thin, gravelly soil that marked where the end of the Precambrian Shield ran close to the surface in this part of the country, into some semblance of a living. The man was known as Duncan "the Night" MacMillan, to distinguish him from all the other Duncan MacMillans in Glengarry County, a society so thick with Scottish immigrants that second names or nicknames were essential for distinguishing among them.

Dad showed this historical account to practically everyone who stopped by the farm and stayed for more than an hour. Years later, he hired a local stonemason and set him to work turning the hunk of granite that sat on the edge of the land our initial reforesting had by now restored into a family monument.

At the top, the stonemason wrote: "They cared for this land." Below it, he etched in "Duncan the Night MacMillan" and, below that, my father's and mother's names and birth dates then, below their names, each one of ours.

When Mum brought Dad's ashes back to the farm from Florida the spring following his death, I cajoled everyone into gathering there, for a makeshift homemade "service" before, by common consent, we buried the ashes at the base of the rock. I can't remember all that was said and done that day, only that someone read from the Bible, and Doug said something by way of a eulogy. His voice was low and intense, and he spoke without notes, trusting the words rising from within him, ending with "He was a good man." Then we emptied the plastic bag of bone bits and fine dust into a shallow hole in the ground at the base of the rock, and covered it up. That done, we turned to each other, arms out. We came together in hugs and, finally, we cried.

Nearly twenty years later, Dick and I had spent a happy hour or so clearing out the weeds that had grown up around the rock, trimming back some of the spruce boughs that leaned down so low they obscured the now lichen-encrusted words. Dick even returned by himself another day to rearrange some rocks that had been dumped by stone pickers nearby, creating almost a circle around the rock, and a couple of rocky ledges on which to sit. And so, that weekend when I came to talk about medical power of attorney, we logically gravitated there. Mugs in hand, we walked up the back lane, taking in the quiet of the early autumn day, remarking on this or that then falling silent. At the rock we settled ourselves comfortably on two of the stones in the circle. I looked at the rock, our lineage and our bonds spelled out in stone.

"So," Dick said, which told me he was ready. I took a breath, feeling it ragged in my chest, thinking of Mum sitting up on her bed waiting for me to make tea. I was aware of a breeze sighing through the spruces and pines, enveloping Dick and me like an ancient blessing, mitigating silence, and our breaking of it here. We talked about the spirit and intent behind putting down limits to medical care for Mum now that she was clearly past the point of being able to enunciate them for herself. We searched for ways to represent Mum's wishes, what she'd wanted when she'd talked about dying in the past. I remembered what she'd told the heart surgeon when he was telling her that the triple-bypass was a risky operation for someone of her age and in her condition: That she didn't care to live if she couldn't carry on with her gardening and her birds. I remembered too what she'd told me the night before the surgery: That she wasn't afraid to die; she'd had a good life. I'd even found an entry in my journal from the previous Christmas when Mum had talked about dying, almost wished for it. We were at my place, sitting by the fire one evening, and she said, "Too bad you can't just will it to happen, like going out the door." I repeated this to my brother, adding what I'd written in my journal at the time; that "I think she is bored with what her life is reduced to now, and wants out."

"Right," Dick said. "Quality of life. If she can't have quality of life ..."

Relief swept through me. We had begun. The old, botched attempt at a living will was behind us now. The timing was right that we should begin again. And "quality of life" was clearly a phrase to use, with an established currency in the medical and legal accounts of such matters. What next? What limits should we, could we set down, and decree? I looked at Dick. This was his turf. Being a doctor, he understood what logically could be considered, because he knew clinically how any such intervention must be calibrated to the body's capacity to respond. For instance, he said, we could stipulate "antibiotics by mouth" but "no intravenous antibiotics" Sitting there on the rock looking out across the field of luxurious late-blooming alfalfa, I listened as Dick explained that if Mum was still strong enough in body and spirit, she'd recover from another bout of pneumonia with the oral antibiotic. Whereas with the intravenous, they use a much stronger class of medications that will treat the illness almost despite the body's recuperative capacity, which often means that another life-threatening event will probably happen soon.

The idea of an advance-care directive is to provide "guidance principles." But for them to take precedence over what a doctor might consider in someone's best interest, they must be clear, and backed with a strong statement reflecting the person's will and self-determination. A person's mere preference, such as not to needlessly prolong life, is not as good as a statement of "deliberate choice," which is considered a "performance" and an "act of will" under the law. So there was a moral point and responsibility in what Dick and I were doing under the shelter of the rock and the trees. We had to use words: precise words, with formal standing in the world.

There was a lovely tenderness in our conversation that morning yet also a certain reserve and careful politeness. For me at least, it was an almost necessary buffer. I was sitting there with my brother discussing not doing this and not doing that in the event of our mother getting really sick. We were drafting a document intended to *not* let others step in to help, *not* to offer all the health care our public system makes freely available to all. We weren't just listing the obvious things like respirators and tube feeding, but subtler, savvy stuff like "pressers" to maintain cardiac output. We were talking about withholding that help, thinking this is what Mum would want: to simply be allowed to die. The politeness and formality were a screen. We talked behind it, masking our actions, hiding our intentions even from our deepest selves, because we were trespassing on her agency; this once fiercely independent person who was "always in the driver's seat of life." We were taking over!

I must have brought something to write on in my jacket pocket. I jotted down some of these things. Then, Dick suggested I type it all up, and email him a draft. He'd suggest any changes, fill in any additional medical elements, and send it back to me. Once we were satisfied with what we'd drafted, I could email it to Doug and Jan, and Doug would frame it as a legal document.

I said that I'd like to run it by Mum first. Dick looked at me. For what it's worth, I said, not feeling like trying to explain my own sense of how things were for Mum. While she was less and less able to engage in the world of abstract words and concepts, I sensed that she was still in there, not just alive to her body and what her body took in, but still working, still trying to figure things out. But I also knew that Mum could no longer readily recognize who Dick was, could no longer call him by name and so for him, perhaps she seemed essentially gone.

"Fine," Dick said now, and that seemed to be that. He swallowed the last of his coffee, glanced across at me. "Ready?"

I stood up, feeling solid and weak at the same time.

"I need a hug," I said. Dick put an awkward arm around me. Sometimes I nudge him a little, asking for a two-armed hug. But this was enough that day, enough for me to ask for and he to give of himself emotionally. We walked back to the farmhouse, talking about this and that then lapsing into companionable silence. And the project moved along. I typed something up, with the preamble stating that Mum had always been a "strong and self-reliant person," that "for her living meant an active independent life," and adding some direct quotes to buttress our claim that this was an expression of her will, not ours. Then I typed the words "Limits to Care," boldfaced and underlined them. I have no memory of what I felt at the time. I think I'd retreated emotionally for the moment, letting the strong arm of my intellect take over.

I can recall speaking to Mum about the document. I had it in my bag when I arrived for my next visit. She greeted me as always: "Ah, there you are," her face blooming into a smile. "Come see the birds," she said, and gestured to her window. It had been a while since she'd even tried to name the birds she watched out her window. "The ducks," she'd say, then "no, geese. Ducks." I'd look and tell her "geese," but still she'd be flustered. Now, she must have meant the chickadees just beyond the west window where her bed was located, a big spruce tree just outside affording privacy for Mum and shelter for the birds. Mum spent hours watching the chickadees, their bright little eyes, and their fluffball bodies playing hopscotch among the branches mere inches from the glass.

I kissed Mum hello and, still holding her hand, joined her in watching the birds at their play outside the window. Then I made tea, brought the tray round to my side of the bed, and handed Mum her cup, glancing down to see that Mum had her hearing aids in. I told her that I'd been down at the farm visiting Dick and his family on the weekend.

"That's nice," Mum said. I told her some of the things we did, the sighting of a deer, the leaves of the maple bush in full fall colour. Mum smiled and nodded as I talked. Then I set my cup to the side, and turned to face her more directly.

"We also talked about you," I said, taking her hand.

"Oh," she said, not quite a question, not passive acknowledgement either.

I told her about the living will, the medical directives we'd talked about. I kept my eyes on Mum's face. She kept her eyes on mine. I felt her hand squeeze mine, and squeezed hers back. I explained about the limits Dick and I were proposing, because, I said, "we don't think you want to be kept alive needlessly." I can't remember whether my voice quavered at the word "you" because the enormity of what this involved was absolutely real to me in that moment. Mum was still looking at me intently. It was as though she was reading my lips and peering right through my eyes. To know if I was sincere, if my heart was pure? Perhaps. Since Mum's death and all the reading I've done since, I now know that Alzheimer's doesn't just take away, but seems to actually give something back. In his book, *The Man Who Mistook His Wife for a Hat and Other Clinical Tales*, Dr. Oliver Sacks reflects on what he's witnessed or been told about people with severe aphasia (loss of language). He recounts hearing a group of patients burst into laughter while watching then-president Ronald Reagan giving a speech on television. Unable to grasp the import, the meaning or content of his words, they were instead listening at an entirely non-verbal level, catching all the "extra-verbal" cues like gestures, tone of voice, rhythm of speech, and inflection. They laughed, Dr. Sacks wrote, because what they heard was Reagan as a phony. Explaining this, Sacks notes that speech isn't just the articulation of cognitive thought. It's "utterance," or as Marshall McLuhan once artfully re-phrased it, "outerance." It is a physical rendering of expression. For people with aphasia, which is a standard feature of dementia, when cognitive communication declines, the capacity for perception in communication at the level of bodily expression seems to increase, he says. The capacity for expressiveness is not only "perfectly preserved," Dr. Sacks writes, it's often also "preternaturally enhanced." He quotes the English neurologist Henry Head, who borrowed the phrase "feeling tone" widely used by African Americans, especially in the South, to name this non-verbal aspect of communication. We're *Homo loquens* before we are *Homo sapiens*, Dr. Sacks suggests, and people with dementia remind us of this in their seeming "inversion, and perhaps a reversion too, to something more primitive and elemental."

They have "an infallible ear for every vocal nuance, the tone, the rhythm, the cadences, the music, the subtlest modulations, inflections, intonations, which can give—or remove—verisimilitude to or from a [person's] voice."

In short, Dr. Sacks writes of the laughing patients he observed, they were "undeceived and undeceivable by words."

I didn't know any of this at the time. I kept talking to Mum as if she could comprehend at least something at some level because that's what my intuition said, and what I wanted to believe. I also did it for myself. I needed to stay connected, to keep my finger on Mum's inner pulse, to steady myself in this journey we were on together. A journey toward death; with this document we were approaching if not entering its border region.

Did Mum realize this too? I have no idea what sense of all this she was making. Only that she kept looking at me hard. When I was finished, she smiled, but said nothing.

"Do you think that's okay?" I asked eventually.

She squeezed my hand again, still looking at me, reading something off my face. She nodded, said something like, "That's fine," and smiled.

I asked if she wanted another cup of tea. "Yes," she said emphatically, and handed me her cup.

By the time I sat down with the director of care at Mum's residence, the document had acquired an addendum from Doug: an existing medical power of attorney, dated January 3, 1996 (the day Dick had come to visit Mum when she was recovering from pneumonia at my house), which Doug had quietly notarized, and filed for future reference. Nothing was said by either Dick or Jan when my supposedly ripped-up document resurfaced. So I took it to the seniors' residence along with the advance care directive. Both the director of care, and the resident doctor were glad, very glad, to have both documents on file.

I came away feeling relaxed. The universe was unfolding, and I was okay with it all. Or so I thought.

I had to be away for a week or so after this. When I returned for my next visit, I saw that Mum's hair had been cut. The lovely upward sweep of the roll in which she'd kept her hair for as long as she'd been my Mum had been replaced by a jagged line of hair falling into her face. She didn't look like Mum at all.

"What happened?" I asked.

"Someone cut it off," Mum said. That's all she knew.

I turned on my heel and went straight to the office. Turns out, the cutting hadn't been done by the resident hairdresser, but by one of the personal-care attendants assigned to help Mum get washed and brushed and dressed in the morning. Something about Mum's hair getting in the way.

I was furious. This was my mother. This was her hair, a hairdo that marked her as much as her name. It was her identity, not something to be done away with for someone else's convenience!

The director apologized. That wasn't good enough. Nothing was good enough. Still, I settled on their giving Mum a free perm at the resident hairdressing salon.

We'd go together. I'd get my hair washed and styled as well. And off we went, arm in arm. Mum and I went to the hairdresser's together, for the first time in our lives. We had a great time.

6

Beginning to Fail

I arrived one day to find Mum sitting up on her bed looking intently out the main, north-facing window. "See the river outside?" she asked. Yes, I said. The glorious Ottawa River does indeed flow by outside the seniors' residence, on the far side of a large city park the treed and grassy grounds of which extend to the road outside Mum's north window. It was spring, misty, and raining, which made it harder to see the river. When I was close enough to kiss Mum hello, she also seemed to be looking at something closer. A car went by. "There," she said.

"That's the road," I said. "The river's there," I said, gesturing.

"Oh," she said, in that tone I'd grown to recognize: not quite a clear aha, because some confusion obviously remained. I can now put names on what was going on: "the referential boundaries of words" breaking down, plus "agnosia," the inability to make meaningful sense of things here and now. Short-term memory loss was eroding the footprint of what's been said so fast that Mum wouldn't even have known that she hadn't said river instead of road. Yet, turning that memory over, I think there was something else. Mum might have been lost in a *terra incognita* relative to what most people recognize as real. But her acute perception and curiosity were still at work. Perhaps with the rain on the asphalt, the road outside Mum's window did become a

river in her mind. Perhaps what she wanted to ask me was, so
what's that car doing sailing by upon it?

But I wasn't informed enough at the time, nor quite relaxed
enough in the moment to just go with Mum's flow, so to speak.
So I directed her attention, appropriately enough I thought, to
the river on the far side of the park, and focused on making tea.
Yet as we sat there in our usual companionable silence, I found
myself inventing the need to cut Mum's nails because her mistaking the road for a river had rattled me. Cutting Mum's nails
gave me comfort. I could snuggle in, pushing my whole arm
under hers as I took her hand in mine and wielded the clippers
with now-practiced ease. I felt her breath on my cheek as she
watched me, inhaled the tea smell on it, and savoured it.

So much of Mum's old life, and her connections to it had
fallen away. She'd read the daily paper when she first moved in.
But now even if I picked up the paper at the desk for her, she
didn't stick with it for long. She couldn't in a way, the words no
longer stayed in her head from one end of the line to the other.
Less and less did. All the stories, the activities and to-do lists that
had anchored her in life were uprooted and gone. The knowledge
and understanding that had tied her into the time of history,
rooted her in the specifics of place, all this was gone too. Her
world hadn't just shrunk. It had disappeared. Her telephone still
sat on her night table, and I knew Jan still regularly called from
Edmonton, engaging Mum in conversation for up to an hour at
a time, she told me later. Mum hardly ever phoned me anymore,
nor I her, because she easily got confused, or annoyed. So, to
avoid the pain and upset, I simply stopped phoning. It was easier
to just show up: "Ah, there you are," Mum always said, and
whether she knew me as Heather or not wasn't an issue, as long
as her eyes lit up when I arrived. When I was leaving, she always

asked, when are you coming back, to which I just said "soon," "Friday" or "next week" having lost all significance. The main thing was that I was part of her world, this small quiet room with the tea things and the plants from Doug on the window sill and the pendulum clock on the wall ticking, chiming away the hours in a perpetual now. The attack on the World Trade Centre in New York and its terrible aftermath were light years away.

I felt as though I was staggering sometimes as I made the transition, the radical shift in time zones, and their different gravitational pulls. I had been working on a new book since 2000, and now, three years later, I was stalled in a second draft. I was less and less able to give speeches too. At the best of times, it always seemed to me to be a huge piece of conjuring, to project words from my mouth with force and passion and logic enough not just to hold the audience's attention but to enlighten them, persuade them, even move them to resolve and action. Recently, though, I'd had one of those panic moments when the words kept coming out of my mouth, but it was like speaking in tongues. I could hear the words in my ear. But my mind could make no sense of them. It was all disconnected. Just words pushed out of me into the air, and my mouthing them helplessly.

It was Mum's falling away from words and what was left in the pauses, the seemingly empty silence, that held my attention now. I was feeling my way into a new way of relating to her, a new way of being with her through the slowed-down senses of touch and smell, my ear more tuned now to cadence than "cognitive" content. I was drawn to this, drawn even to the anguish of it, as if feeling the pain of all that was being lost were essential to my gaining a foothold in what was left to be discovered. It was as though I had to fully live and experience the gradual disappearance of Mum's identity. Not just to get past denial, but to open myself to what or where she was going now. I felt that I was in some rite of passage, another stage in my growing up. My bones themselves had to shift. And so I ached for this woman whose face was forgetting the feel of the sun and the wind and the rain, whose feet no longer stepped boldly across the floor, with a decisive click of her high heel; they meekly shuffled now, the soles of her flat shoes rarely raised above the nap of the rug, the bland flat of the linoleum in the hall. Her hands had always been busy, true to her nickname Beaver. They'd always been dirt-stained and gnarled from the hours she spent wielding her spade in the garden, her hammer and saw making and fixing innumerable things. Now those hands lay pale and idly loose in her lap.

"I'm getting old," she commented one visit. "Worse than last year."

"Yes, perhaps," I said, feeling a thud of affirmation deep in my chest, the flutter of fear at what "worse" might entail and, with it, my private, secret fear: Could I stay the course? I grew used to the cycle, the curtaining over in the moment of impact, the ache surfacing at three o'clock in the morning as I struggled to admit this latest revelation, this confirmation of ground giving way. I was letting the unknown of death and dying make its approach, I think, letting mortality itself worm its way into the joints and bones of my being.

One summer day I arrived more tired than usual. I had been pushing myself to get on with the book; for the first time in my life, I had missed a deadline. I had also just come from the hospital where the doctors wanted to re-admit Donald. My son had initially refused, and we had spent a hot hour or so walking about on the hospital grounds with me trying to stay calm and reasonable, and Donald finally agreeing to let the specialists try something else. Plus, my separation from Miles had gone ahead, and I was left to sell our ex-marital home, and having to live in it too, month after month, while waiting for a buyer.

It felt good just to sit next to Mum, feeling the warmth from her arm and shoulder mingle with the warmth from mine. I told her the latest on Donald and she squeezed my hand. "That's too bad." And then we sat together in silence. At one point I knew she would focus on her teacup and comment on what a lovely cup it was. And I would agree. I did agree and forever will agree, her intonation of "lovely" sounding to me then and forever like a Venetian glassblower pronouncing sheer perfection into the air. Then, after the customary pause, she leaned in for a kiss, fully and satisfyingly on the mouth. I didn't get up as I usually did after putting the cups back on the tray when the teapot was empty. Instead, I thought, why not? I slumped down lower in the bed, snuggled my head against Mum's shoulder, and closed my eyes.

"Don't mind me," I said, feeling totally at ease.

"I don't," she said. I felt something brush the top of my head; her lips perhaps, and I dozed off.

After my snooze, I got up and busied myself with the usual routines. I washed out the teacups in the bathroom and put them away, dumped the teabags in the toilet, rinsed the teapot out and put it away, aware that Mum was quietly watching me as I worked. Then she stood up and put her arms around me.

"I love you very much," she said, her voice vibrant, almost trembling with emotion. Her eyes were shiny with tears.

"I love you very much too," I said, hearing my voice crack as full-throttle feeling poured through me as well. We stood there hugging each other hard—for the first time in our lives as far as I can remember. She'd never said "I love you" to me before; nor really had I to her.

I put the dog on her leash and left the building, got into my car, and just sat there in the late-day sunlight, feeling stunned and amazed. I'd waited all my life for this; maybe Mum had too.

For years I'd had Margaret Laurence's Hagar from *The Stone Angel* in my mind as my sort of dying wish for my mother. I desperately hoped that, like Hagar, my mother would put aside her proud, withholding self-sufficiency, would break the shackles of wilful self-control, and experience a Hagar-like epiphany, surrendering herself to life, to love, and to the joy that comes in feeling this fully. I had put feeling love for Marvin, the son who had taken care of her over the years and whom she had taken for granted second, since I was the Marvin stand-in, and I didn't want to appear self-serving even to myself. In fact I didn't see myself as part of the picture at all. Nor did I imagine how much my taking myself and my needs out of the picture was perpetuating the pattern. I saw this purely as a change I wanted for Mum but a change for her to make, though maybe I could prod it along a bit by getting Mum to talk about her emotions, her mother's death for example. I never imagined that if I changed, she could too. Sitting in the car that day, watching the late-afternoon sun dapple the space in which I was parked, I marvelled at how I might have been breaking a few shackles of my own, coming down off a barn roof I'd never been aware I was up on.

When I spoke to friends about my mother, I invariably told them about her own mother's tragic death, just as Mum was recovering from nearly a year in bed with scarlet fever. I usually also explained, in my best voice of compassionate understanding of course, how she had taught herself some powerful coping lessons, essentially to hold herself aloof, duly disguised behind blood-red lipstick, to never really trust anyone else not to abandon her like her mother had done so precipitously when she was nine. I either said or suggested that I didn't expect much from my mother. Nonetheless, mature person that I prided myself on being, I was okay with that.

I'd begun to let go the day I took those photos at Mum's old house when I was clearing it out. But that was only the beginning, getting rid of the baggage, taking down the barriers of my own withholding. It had taken a long time since, more than a year, to reach this point, where I let myself go at last, giving way to the simple human need for love and comfort, from my mother. The kiss on the top of my head, the long, deep hug, the "I love you very much," the tears brightening her eyes had been the result.

My argument with Doug about what was really going on with Mum had drifted into a silence between us. The point for Doug, still, was that Mum hadn't consciously chosen to change, of her own free will. It was Alzheimer's that had changed her, stripping away her normal inclination to control and judge, to treat love as a scarce resource, parcelled out for good behaviour. And so any affection offered by her now didn't really count, because she wasn't consciously in control of bestowing it. But maybe that wasn't the point, I thought now. Maybe Mum wasn't the point: we were, each of her children in turn, letting go of past hurts as necessary. For me at least, the point was that I could change, and that could change everything.

Sitting in the car that day, idly stroking the dog's head as she rested it on my knee, I realized that it wasn't just about Mum and her choices. It was about me and mine. Having chosen to be there for Mum as she went down and out of this world, and driven too by my not having been there for my father, the consequences followed. At a time when Mum was no longer capable of roles and performance and self-mastery, I had put roles and performance aside, and allowed myself to just be. In the cradle of my mother's body, my head resting against the bony knob of her shoulder, I crossed into a new way of being.

By now, I had grown tired of the scientific literature I had read when first trying to justify moving Mum into a home, getting her away from me essentially and into the safe hands of professionals. I discovered a second literature on aging and dementia, a broader, more social-context than clinical approach that focuses on the whole person experiencing the dementia rather than the "deficits" associated with a disease category, which is so central to the "medical-model" approach. The social-context approach also widens the frame of reference on what self and person involves from the isolated individual to the larger social situations through which we articulate our human existence. Selfhood remains intact, Steven Sabat argues in *The Experience of Alzheimer's Disease: Life Through a Tangled Veil*. But to grasp this, you have to be open, and choose to be open, to the flux and continuity between one self and another in everyday life. In other words, open to considering that the "I think therefore I am" free agent could be just the tip of the iceberg of who we are, and what remains, therefore, when Alzheimer's has ravaged a person's thinking, judging, planning, and capacity for logic and coherent discourse. Identity is a social construction, not just because our personal identity depends in part on how we are treated and perceived, but because personal identity is bound up in social identity, the social self that emerges in a social situation. It emerges according to Sabat, "in the dynamic interplay of mutual recognition of one's own and another person's position in the social situation. . . . Put another way . . . , it would be impossible to manifest the persona of a helpful parent without the recognition and cooperative behaviour of one's child."

I think back to when my son Donald was an infant and the rich interplay of smiles and baby talk through which we passed our time together as I laboured determinedly to bond with him in a way I felt Mum hadn't succeeded with me and perhaps my other siblings as well. In a sense, Donald and I called each other into existence in that first phase of our social existence, as mother and child. Of course, I wasn't thinking this at the time; I was hardly thinking at all. I just remember snuffling my face against my baby's soft tummy when I was drying him after a bath, or after changing his diaper, and how he snuffled his face against me, not just my breasts when nursing, but my neck, my shoulder. I remember too how we played peekaboo with the baby blankets, the split-second timing of our glances, the delight in his eyes when his gaze latched onto mine.

One journal entry from when he was a few months old chronicles his first experiments with language: "He lets out one of his melodic screeches. His eyes are searching for mine, a smile ready as I turn to look. I smile. He immediately grins. He makes another *aeyee* sound. I smile again. He grins again, this time producing another *aeyee* as he grins. He's got it figured, the connection between the sounds his throat and tongue can project and our smiling at each other across the room." We were still attuned to each other in a dance of connection even if we weren't physically skin-to-skin.

I think of child psychoanalyst Joyce McDougall who, at a 1992 "Sleeping, Dreaming and Dying" conference re-phrased the biblical dogma, "In the beginning was the word" into "In the beginning was the voice, and even in the [womb]. . . . sound and rhythm." I think too of George Herbert Mead stressing the biological roots of social interaction. He postulated that before there is the "vocal gesture" of the spoken, properly articulated word, there is simply the gesture expressing emotion and arousing emotion in others, first evidenced, he writes in *Mind, Self and Society*, in the "common social act involved in the care of the child." More recently, child psychologists and linguists have emphasized the "kinesthetic rhythm" of pre-verbal communication, and how this encompasses both physical games like peekaboo and pat-a-cake to baby talk, with its singsong rhythms and its strong "emotional content," enticing the infant forward into the world of play and conversation, into becoming a member of society.

"Emotional content": In other words, love. Love flowing like a river of mutual meaning-making, carrying cars and who knows what else on its current; flowing too in that moment after I'd told my mother about my difficult time with my son that day, when I let my stressed-out body simply subside against my mother's age-shrivelled one, and received the blessing of her lips on top of my head as I drifted off to sleep.

Neuroscientists using brain-scanning machines have discovered a whole network of neurons that seem to explain actions of mutual identification not only in humans but also in animals. According to J. Madeleine Nash's Canadian *Time* magazine article, "The Gift of Mimicry," these "mirror neurons" have the capacity to "resonate with the emotional state of others." It's not necessarily an innate capacity although scientists think that the distinctive web of connections linking neurons in the motor and sensory systems with the "limbic" systems responsible for visceral and emotional responses are present at birth. Nevertheless, it's thought they are activated and expanded through experience. The article describes how when a baby smiles and the mother smiles back, "the brain sets up a circuit linking the motor system that turns up the corners of the baby's mouth to the visual image of the smiling mother to the emotional state we call happiness." Moreover, Nash maintains that "there are multiple if still tenuous lines of evidence to suggest that neural networks with mirror properties may be responsible for the empathetic response that forms the root of social behaviour. They may also help explain how human language emerged from the more primitive communication systems of monkeys and apes." Neuroscientists think the key is the bridge between movement and meaning these neurons provide because another's actions aren't just observed, they're entered into by way of mirror neurons in the somatosensory cortex. It's seemingly the same with sound, particularly the non-word elements of "prosody," the musical tone and tempo of human speech—what the article describes as its "emotional contours." In other words, "feeling tone."

I have always worked well with words, conjuring with them, thrusting and parrying with them, building bridges of refined intellectual understanding even in instances when a simple nod or embrace would have done. And so when I read Betsy Warland's observation in *Bloodroot*, her exquisite meditation on mother-loss: "To exist, language must separate itself from what it seeks to articulate. In the process, it separates us"—I felt a long-withheld truth hitting home. This might explain my journey into writing: an alibi for staying separate and aloof so much of my life. Now I realized that there was another, equally bittersweet truth to be found as well. As Alzheimer's hacked away language as a workable bridge between Mum and me, this more primal stuff, the tactile give and take of love's physical connections, was there to hold us both as I slumped and dozed on her shoulder that day. Not just because the science of "mirror neurons" says so, but because I made that choice. I stepped onto the bridge of inter-dependent connection, trusting that it would hold me.

It wasn't intellectual understanding that prompted these breakthroughs, nor learning about "existential phenomenology" and its importance in finding one's way through the seeming wasteland of dementia and toward the border regions of death. It took another, more intuitive intelligence, an openness to contemplate what my senses were taking in, an attentiveness fierce enough for my body to coin a language in response to what it all meant. It was as unconscious as when I'd spontaneously coined various rhythmic phrases when talking to my infant son, and just as urgent.

Surrender, I thought as I sat in the car that day, the sun now sunk behind the hedge, the dog lying down with her muzzle touching my leg. The verb can move two ways: "surrendering" in the sense of letting go of something that while burdensome, is nonetheless familiar; and "surrender" in the sense of letting in, letting down the guard. Giving up, and giving over. Opening the gate, and surrendering to whatever will come. Nor was this surrender simply a choice. It was a struggle. Now as I sat in the car outside Mum's residence, I sensed that somehow I had come through to the other side and arrived at a state of being open to come what may.

I got there without any of the available literature. I got there on pure intuition, and longing: longing to be in touch, to stay in touch, to love and to be loved. It ushered me into "a level of communication that is not coded, that is beyond words," as my friend, the architect Judith Roux put it to me once, describing her own journey into being there with her mother when she was dying. It also brought me into the realm of what I'd call "spirit talk," uttered from the depths of pure being through the medium of touch and gaze, and the sound of the engaged voice rather than what the mind is trying to articulate through it. The medium was the flow of intonation rather than words themselves, the pure loving energy of call and response.

I think now that this has a lot to say to the literature on communications theory, which in turn has a lot to say to the literature on Alzheimer's, and its treatment. Through my scholarly interest and involvement in communication studies, I've known that mainstream theory primarily sees communication as information transmission, with the focus on efficient communication channels and keeping the content free from interference. The romantic in me has long been drawn to the older conceptions of communication, what theorist James Carey calls the "ritual" model, which is more concerned with social bonding than information transactions. However, I now feel most comfortable with the more recent, some might say "postmodern" approach, which considers communication ecologically, as embedded in relationships and inseparable from the context or environment. This is what Marshall McLuhan was getting at when he coined his famous aphorism "the medium is the message." He meant that whatever medium we use in communicating with each other itself fundamentally shapes what comes across. Most of the theorists I've read on this have focused on what we normally think of as "mass media" of communication—television versus radio, print versus the Internet—and have contrasted the effects of printed paper as a medium versus radio waves and electronic bits.

But the first medium is the body itself, in keeping with the roots of "language" being in the body, as the French word *langue*, meaning "tongue," reminds us. In 2000, I wrote in *The Gazette: International Journal of Communications* that the first "line" of communication is the umbilical chord. If I were to continue this trajectory now, which I didn't dare do at the time, I'd say that while the cord was surgically severed at birth, the flow of communication from my body to my son's continued without interruption, as I nursed him at my breast, as I rocked him in my arms, as I engaged in a host of pre-verbal rhythmic sounds, enunciated from a well of pure instinct and love. All of that attentiveness and responsiveness created a medium or social environment that helped draw Donald into the world of spoken communication. In the shelter of our home, my husband Miles and I conjured an ecological matrix that pulsed with the same kind of rhythms as the flow of blood that had nourished his growth inside my womb.

I don't think I got much of this in the first year or so of my life. Not only was I bottle fed instead of nursed at the breast, Mum was bedridden after my birth, and I was cared for at least in part by a stranger: a nurse called Anna who was just beginning to learn English. However, in this last year or so of Mum's life, I think that she and I made up for this in the environment we created during my visits, which served as the medium of our communication. Maybe with my taking over many actions, like making and pouring the tea, it looked as though I was leading, setting the pace. But the point of seeing communication ecologically, through the to-and-fro of relationships, is that no one thing or person leads. The relationship itself leads. In other words, that afternoon on Mum's bed, the act of Mum and I leaning toward each other led.

And as our evolving relationship led, it took me far beyond the realm of quantifiable knowing and meaning-making into an awareness of meaning beneath the surface of words and even the need for words. It opened me to the subtle flow of pure feeling, pure spirit. Somewhere along the way too, Mum and the meaningfulness of her life with "severe dementia" was no longer framed solely around her and her capabilities as a free agent. It had been re-framed around us, and our relating to each other. I think about Dr. Denis Noble's speculation in *The Music of Life: Biology Beyond the Genome* that perhaps "the self is an integrative construct," even "an integrative process," embedded in a larger "semantic context" which, he elaborated in an email, include "the networks of social and cultural life." Given how much Mum's and my relating to each other and making meaning together was a network of give and take, a sometimes seamless ebb and flow of gesture and eye contact, I'd say there's truth in what he's saying. And I'm content to leave it hovering there, inconclusive, yet suggestive and mysterious. But I like the notion that when the mind of someone with dementia declines, it does so within the nest of relationships which can carry on sustaining and nurturing it. What once emerged in the context of loving social engagement, begins to submerge in the dementia of old age, but is not gone altogether as long as the relationships hold.

A month or two later, something in Mum seemed to shift. I couldn't put my finger on it, except that when I arrived for tea, I often found her curled up on her bed, not quite asleep but close. "Oh, there you are," she always said, her face blossoming into a smile when I made a noise loud enough to rouse her. She reached for her hearing aids and glasses, and sat up, hands happily empty in her lap and waited for me to make our tea. She was losing weight, I was sure and, indeed, the staff reported that she was less and less interested in eating. She'd begin with soup, and tea of course, and end with her customary bowl of ice cream. But she often now didn't eat her main course. I phoned Doug, who still regularly fetched her home to his place for Sunday supper. Had he noticed any change? Not particularly, he said. So when I phoned Dick and Jan, I kept it light, mostly just asking when they were next coming for a visit. I didn't want to seem alarmist by saying something like "she's beginning to fail" or "taking a turn for the worse." Plus, I was too close to Mum myself to see what was happening in such definitive, categorical terms. The messages I was getting, or tapping into were more akin to the intelligence associated with water divining. The message, such as it is, comes through the fresh-cut apple or willow bow held tight against the palm of the hand; the turning is instinctive, the sap's response to water pulsing through the earth. It's as though I had found Mum's larger pulse. Not just with my finger either. My whole being had found it, had tuned in. I didn't realize how, at the same time as I was being drawn into this intimate inward attunement, I was drifting away from my siblings, particularly Doug and my only sister, Jan.

Jan came from Edmonton in mid-August, and decided she'd take Mum down to Mum's old home on the Rideau River, which, happily we'd been in no rush to sell. Her plan was to spend the bulk of her visit alone there with Mum. I didn't know it at the time, but Jan had done some hard thinking of her own after being with Mum at our father's terrible death nearly twenty years ago. She'd decided that she didn't want to go through an ordeal like that again, and so she didn't particularly want to be there when Mum passed away. When she came that summer, therefore, she had in her mind that this might be goodbye. So her focus was fully and completely on Mum, wanting to sit with her, holding her hand, finding her own way in to Mum's essential pulse. She didn't particularly want or need to have me around.

I didn't get it at the time. I didn't know it either; Jan only told me years later. So I was hurt at how she seemed to brush me off. I brought Donald down to the cottage on a day release from the hospital—as a buffer? Perhaps. Though I also wanted her to tell me how much better he was. But she was no more interested in focusing on Donald than on me. "I like his haircut," she told me, and that was about it. Or at least all that registered, because I'd been hoping and waiting for the chance to fill her in on Mum, really. Then, I imagined, we could talk a little about what to expect, and maybe grieve a little, sister to sister. But her focus was just on Mum, and mine on her, pleasing my big sister, gauging her mood, not mine. I never considered my own need to confide, to share, and come together. It was clear to me too that Jan relied on Dick's assessment for a larger picture of where Mum stood. After all, he was the doctor in the family. Perhaps, too, his more clinical approach suited her better than my more emotive one. She once called me the "emotion queen" in the family. I could understand all this, intellectually, but intellectual understanding was beside the point, especially when everything was shifting, the old family patterns breaking up. During spring break-up, water long held down by sheets of grinding ice surges up between the rupturing cracks, glistening like dark muscle, seeking nothing except release. Nobody can escape that imperative force, nor deny it through decorous politeness.

I could have made a move, could have changed the pattern of how we related to each other. I could have simply opened my mouth, spoken my feelings out loud, told her how much I needed her. But I didn't. Not a word about my fears, my needs. No slumping against her shoulder

We had some good times together anyway. Jan had brought her camera, and took lots of pictures, including one of me with my forehead pressed against Mum's, our fingers interlaced the way they naturally moved together at this time. I in turn took lots of pictures of Jan with Mum as well. And when we drove Mum back to the residence prior to Jan catching her flight back to Edmonton, we got one of the aides to take a picture of us both squished together on either side of Mum on her bed. I treasure it still, the last picture I have of Mum before she died. She looks like an old woman alright: her short hair sparse, white and light as angel wings around her ears. Her waxy and pale face sets her dramatically apart from Jan and me with our summer-tanned cheeks. Still, there's a big happy smile on her face; she's vibrantly alive and engaged. And she's gesturing, as though trying to introduce Jan and I, and I can remember that she said the word "daughter"—whether with an "S" or not, I can't recall; nor by then did it matter.

I brought Mum to the cottage one more time, over the Labour Day weekend when Dick came with his family for a visit. By then, Mum was clearly failing. She still liked to sit by the river in her old lounge chair with its faded patchwork of patches and restitching, the one I'd photographed two years ago during the long time out I'd taken from my cleanup frenzy. But she found it harder and harder to stay awake, or to hold her attention on the life on the water, the birds flitting here and there, the boats going by. Perhaps too she simply had trouble holding her head up by then, all her muscles were wasting away. In fact, her skin hung so loose on her frame, I imagined that she could shrug it off at any moment.

I looked out the window every so often to see if Dick was still sitting with Mum and talking to her. Sometimes he was still there, but Mum's head had fallen forward onto her chest. Sometimes I looked out, and Mum was sitting there by herself, Dick's chair empty. I couldn't blame him for walking off to find something that needed doing, fixing, something to grab hold of because Mum couldn't really remember who he was. Dick, her last-born, her baby! "Dickie-boy," she used to call him.

Mum was having trouble knowing who her first-born was too, though she saw him often. She sometimes now called Doug "Dad," mistaking him for her father, Douglas Bayne. And indeed there was a strong resemblance, not just in looks but also in incisive intellect and charming personality. But that wouldn't have mattered, I knew, from the few times Mum had mistakenly called me Janet.

The weekend was hard for Mum too. It wasn't just how weakness and fatigue had drastically scaled back what she was capable of doing, how much space she could even navigate. The place she'd called home for nearly twenty years no longer held her in its familiar rooms and furnishings. The familiar had turned strange, and Mum was clearly lost; not comforted, but anxious in her old home. Her room in the residence meant home to her now. And so I plugged in extra night lights when we all went to bed, and put a bucket in Mum's room, joking that this was her "honey bucket" from childhood and our days at the farm when all we had was the outhouse at the bottom of the hill behind the house.

I remember seeing my father at the farm when he was recovering from the last terrible round of chemotherapy and the oncologist had given him a 70/30 chance. That is, a 30 per cent chance of living, a 70 per cent chance of dying. We were alone in the house together, and I found him in the living room, sitting in his thick fall jacket with a blanket around his shoulders, hunched over and withdrawn into himself by the fire. I brought a chair and sat close to him. I wanted to break the silence, step into the abyss and say something like "you're dying, eh Dad?"

But I couldn't. I hadn't the courage, or I wanted to protect my father, or myself. Still, I did manage to open my mouth and speak, saying I had the impression that he had "crossed over." In Dad's case, cancer was eating him up. Death was making an aggressive, obvious approach, quantifiable in statistical probabilities. With Mum, it was infinitely subtle, like twilight deepening into darkness, the colours that distinguish objects leeched away, an absence of light encroaching. Still, some instinct told me that Mum too was beginning to cross over.

After Dick and his family left, I made us a last cup of tea before taking Mum back to the residence. As I waited for the water to boil, and set everything on the tray, I kept glancing to check on her outside. I saw her head nod and finally sink onto her chest. I watched her snow-white hair flitting this way and that in the breeze off the water. It was the only sign of animation above the blanket I had tucked in around her despite the warmth of the day.

Less than a month later, Mum got pneumonia. I'd been away in Vancouver, to meet with my editor and to give a speech. Both perhaps; I can't remember. I returned to find a message on my machine to call the residence; Mum wasn't well. When I got there, she was curled up on her bed, one hand tucked under her cheek, the other scrunched close to her chest. She didn't stir when I made my usual arrival noises by the bed. I walked around to the other side so I could look into her face. I bent low, calling her name quietly. She opened her eyes.

"Ah, there you are," she said softly. She smiled, and lifted an arm. "Come," she said, shifting over to make room for me on the bed.

It was nothing by now for me to do such a thing. I slipped off my shoes, and slid into the space Mum had made beside her. I snuggled close, the skin of my forehead cool against the feverish skin of hers. Sigh. I think it was a mutual sigh. Mum looked at me, her hazel eyes bright, though blurred at such close quarters. I closed my eyes, and let myself drift. I'd taken the red-eye special back to Ottawa, and then barely had time to shower and change before heading to the university to teach for three hours straight. All through the class, my mind kept hearing what they'd said on the phone when I called in: that Mum had pneumonia. At the same time, I had to hold in my mind all the threads of the classroom dialogue, had to push myself just to speak in coherent sentences and even then, hearing them come out thin and flat. At least Donald was out of the hospital now and getting back on his feet. I'd check in with him later.

Meanwhile, as I wrote in my journal that night, "It was so nice at last to simply lie there with Mum, warm body curled toward warm body," feeling her hot breath on my face, my breath overlapping with hers.

Eventually Mum stirred and said that her mouth was dry.

I opened my eyes. "Tea?"

She smiled, "That would be nice." And so we had tea, which I took to be a good sign. In fact, when I suggested it, she thought she might even go in for supper. And so we ventured down the short distance of hall to the small, plain dining room where all the people who need help eating, or moving, or finding their way are brought together to eat or to be fed. As usual, we walked arm in arm, our fingers laced, and if Mum leaned a little more on me this time, neither of us cared to comment. Mum also used the handrail along the wall for support, something she'd disdained to do when she moved onto the floor.

We arrived at the doorway to the little dining room where the attendant would get Mum seated and tie a bib around her neck.

"That was a good walk," I told Mum brightly.

"A good stagger," she replied, and we smiled at each other.

She's on the mend, I thought. Still, since Deanna, the care director was still in her office as I passed, I took a moment to check in with her on Mum. She told me what antibiotics Mum was on, and also that they were worried about her becoming mal-nourished. So they'd started to give her Ensure, a canned nutritional supplement that comes in a choice of vanilla, banana or strawberry. They'd given my father Ensure when the poison from chemotherapy had scoured his once-robust body and taken his appetite away. Now they were giving the supplement to my mother, which surely told me something.

Yes, I said when Deanna asked about payment, just put it on the bill, and Janet, my sister, would pay. I took a breath, and mentioned the medical care directive, and of the residence's promise that, if it came to it, Mum would be allowed to stay in the residence until she died. Yes, Deanna said, Mum could stay on, unless she was to break or fracture a bone. Yes, I said; that was understood. She'd have to be hospitalized then.

In the morning, Mum's fever was down, and the pneumonia subsided nicely. Two weeks later, she developed a urinary-tract infection. This is to be expected with people being kept in adult diapers. The doctor gave her antibiotics, and this nominally cured her, but left her at a slightly lower level of normal. I continued to make tea when I came, and we continued to sit side by side on her bed drinking it. I told her about my day, and periodically, she said, "Oh yes" or "That's nice." I remarked about the chickadees outside, and she said, "Very nice" and "Lovely." We took turns agreeing that each of our cups was lovely to look at. And then we sat in comfortable silence, the pendulum wall clock ticking beside us. She still leaned in for a kiss, but I noticed that even these muscles were getting weaker. I stroked the soft skin between her thumb and forefinger, and she did the same to me. And so September drifted into October, and I marvelled at how our tea ritual held us—as the rituals of mass have been found to hold others with severe, late-stage dementia. Dr. Sacks writes of such a man in *The Man who Mistook his Wife for a Hat*: "I saw an intensity and steadiness of attention and concentration that I had never seen before in him or conceived him capable of … the perfect alignment of his spirit with the spirit of the Mass…. He was wholly held, absorbed, by a feeling."

One day, Mum held up the teacup I'd just handed her.

"I'm supposed to drink out of this?"

"Yes, Mum," I said. "That's the cup," and I took a sip from mine.

"Ah," she said, and followed suit.

Another day, we were sitting there quietly, the only sound being her clock on the wall near her bed, and she said, "See that shiny thing going back and forth?"

I could tell she meant the pendulum of the clock reflected in the mirror on the wall opposite us. Yes, I said, and was about to name it as I was still in the habit of doing. But Mum spoke first.

"Isn't it lovely?" she asked.

The word pendulum lodged in my throat, suddenly utterly irrelevant. I swallowed hard then nodded. Yes, I said, squeezing Mum's hand. "It is lovely to look at," just for what it is, without a name or understood function.

Lovely, just in itself.

7

The call came on a sunny Saturday afternoon: Mum had fallen getting out of bed. I got the message when I returned from grocery shopping, and immediately thought: now what? I even wondered if this might be a message left over from yesterday. When Mum had woken up on Friday, she didn't want to get out of bed. She didn't feel well, she told the attendant who'd come to help her dress. A little dizzy, that's all; she just wanted to be left alone. Instead, they rushed her to the local hospital, the Queensway Carleton, in an ambulance. I'd been tied up at the time, and my sister-in-law Norma had gone to be there and find out what was what. She called me later saying they still had Mum under observation, but there didn't seem to be anything wrong; Mum's hemoglobin was a little low, correctable with iron pills, that's all. Norma didn't mind staying on; she'd take Mum back to the residence too. Good, I thought, feeling so glad to leave it to good, kind Norma, almost a second sister to me over the years, not just another in-law. I can't remember what was going on in my life just then. Too much on my plate as usual; plus a new relationship I thought I was happily in the throes of had just dead-ended, leaving me confused, insecure, depressed, and just plain tired of it all—all the things I had to do, trying to do my best for Mum, and my son's illness appearing to be chronic, requiring ongoing treatment. It got to be too much sometimes.

So I wasn't particularly thinking of Mum, just me, poor me, as I got back into my car and headed to the residence. I hadn't called first because I didn't trust myself not to be rude. I arrived to discover that they'd gone ahead and sent Mum to the hospital in an ambulance. Not again, I thought. Who's paying for it, I thought. The nurse in charge that day explained that Mum might have fractured her hip. Oh, I said. The nurse handed me Mum's hearing aids; Mum hadn't put them in that morning. I got out a "thanks," shoved them in my purse, and left.

I steamed through the doorway to emergency to find the waiting room full. I scanned the scene looking for Mum's familiar white hair, her age-shrunken body held as upright as she could still manage. I went to the desk, the nurse checked her chart, and pointed. Mum was still on an ambulance gurney, and a bunch of these were lined up in the hall. I found Mum easily enough. She was chatting with the ambulance attendant, a tall, dark, and very handsome young man. Flirting with him is more like it. Her eyes were bright, her cheeks flushed. Yes, definitely flirting, I thought, and the young man was smiling, clearly charmed by her in turn.

"Ah, there you are," Mum said when I came close. I leaned in to kiss her, and she kissed me back. It felt like I'd arrived at a party. I turned to the young man for an update. A fractured hip, I thought, was surely not as bad as a broken one. He thought it might be a false alarm and Mum would be fine. I said thanks, and he wandered off to find his buddies attending other gurneys that day.

I got Mum some tea at the hospital's Tim Horton's, and we settled down to wait. But as one hour became two, it was clear that Mum was in pain.

"Why does it hurt?" she kept asking, *sotto voce* so as not to appear complaining, not to make a fuss. I bent over the side of the gurney, holding one of her hands in one of mine, and used the other to stroke the hair back from her face. I told her that she'd fallen; she might have fractured her hip. Where? she asked. My face close, I told her: back in her room at the residence. She nodded and lay still for a while, then asked again, "Why does it hurt so much?" And once again I told her, my hand holding hers, she giving it a squeeze and I squeezing back.

This went on and on, her moaning softly, then her eyes searching for mine, me leaning in close, stroking her face, squeezing her hand, telling her what had happened, telling her where it had happened, hearing her say "ah," feeling her squeeze my hand, her eyes glued to mine.

"Fused" I called it in my journal later. "The two of us were fused to each other," at times, almost literally as I rested my forehead against hers. I was aware of my back aching as I bent over the railing of the gurney, but the pain was somewhere off in left field, poking away trying to get my attention, but failing. My friend, singer-songwriter Pat Mayberry whose day job is as a social worker in palliative care, once spoke to me of "channelling as communication; channelling energy," and I think that's what I was doing with Mum that day. What both of us were doing. I was submerged in it, in the flow of communing between us, the pain in my back immaterial. Equally, while I was aware of it, I didn't pay attention to the ache in my right arm from stretching so that I could stroke Mum's cheek while, with my left hand I held her right one, absorbing her pain as best I could.

"Why does it hurt?"

"You might have fractured your hip."

"Where?"

"In your room . . ."

"Ah," and a tightening of our fingers in each other's hand. I smoothed back her hair, stroked her temple and, again and again, answered the same questions as if for the first time. And so we continued in a sort of minuet of private time as two hours became three. A nurse or someone would come past the gurneys, taking first one and then another way. I asked the nurse each time: How much longer? Finally a different one, the triage nurse, I subsequently learned, came by for a look, and called out loudly as she returned to her post: "That woman is in excruciating pain." Soon we were in; they had an examining room ready. And, as easily as water finding its way among roots and rocks, I came along too.

Sure enough, when the nurse came into the examining room, she gave me my cue to leave, to go on out to the main waiting room while she undressed Mum and did all the vital-signs work that is required. But it didn't make any sense for me to budge, and so I didn't. I don't think I explained about Mum's Alzheimer's either; I wasn't thinking that clearly or rationally. I just kept my eyes fixed on Mum's as the pain came at her, savagely now, with every little move involved in the undressing.

"It's okay, it's okay. The doctor will give you something for the pain soon," I kept saying, a mantra I'd been repeating for at least an hour by then. I kept holding Mum's hand, and she squeezed it hard as she rode out each wave of pain. "Ah, Mum," I said, again and again, my eyes on hers as we got first her cardigan sweater off, then her blouse, then the navy blue pants—mercifully the ones with an elasticized waist, though the waistband snagged on Mum's hip, and she cried out loud for the first time, tears erupting in her eyes.

When the doctor came he seemed a little startled to see me, but didn't order me out, which is just as well as I might have taken him on—not just with words, but with fingernails and teeth, I was that viscerally engaged. Mum's pain had stripped me too, down to basic instinct. I needed to be at her side; she needed me here too. It was as simple and non-negotiable as that.

The doctor took less than a minute to pronounce the verdict: broken hip, which I was a little shocked to learn was another way of saying "fractured hip." He'd call in a surgeon for a consult; the man should arrive within the hour, the doctor said. I waited for him to go on, to what Mum and I were waiting for: pain medication now! Mum was being stoic, so I reminded him, politely enough I hope. He disappeared out the back door of the examining room, into the inner sanctum of the emergency room, returning with a needle. Finally! I'd stayed beside Mum's head the whole time, leaning in to explain as the doctor was about to examine her by lifting her leg. "It's going to hurt a little," I told her, and held fast as she squeezed my hand hard. Now I told her the doctor was about to give her something for the pain. She nodded, accepting that the needle would hurt a little too. "It'll feel better soon," I said, Mum nodded and even smiled a bit at the doctor.

"Thank you," she said, her charm and sense of decorum shining through.

They wheeled Mum into one of the curtained cubicles that ring the main action in emergency. As the sedation set in, Mum dozed off, and I was free to look around. So here we are, I thought; home is here. It was as clear as that. For one thing, I had no energy to think too far into the future; for another, I was submerged in the ebb and flow of the immediate now. Someone brought a bagged lunch. I drank the thin orange juice and bit hungrily into the sandwich. As I munched, I watched the action around the still-hectically busy emergency ward, and was struck at how calm it was beneath the surface. In fact, when I wrote to the hospital afterward, thanking them for all they'd done, I shared my hunch that there was a lot of continuity of staff here. Because what held the chaos together, despite a welter of doctors, nurses, and orderlies coming and going, was the eye contact among them. There'd be a noise, a voice raised in pain or alarm, and instantly the staff made eye contact around the open space. Sometimes I saw a hand come down briefly on a shoulder in passing, or someone stepped across the room to lend a hand with something. It was all done so smoothly, suggesting trust and rapport, and a still-thriving ethic of compassion among all the gadgets and machines.

When the bone surgeon arrived, we leaned our elbows on the steel railings along the side of Mum's bed. Having been together through the day so far, I didn't want to leave Mum now, and consult about the risks and reasons for corrective surgery in another room. Still, Mum hadn't put in her hearing aids when I arrived earlier, and could only hear if you stooped down close to her ear. So she probably missed a lot of the discussion. I did too, because I didn't understand fully what the operation would involve, beyond anaesthetic, which posed its own risks to a body as frail as Mum's. The hospital provided a phone for me to call Dick in Montreal. He explained the procedure in slightly more prosaic terms. But the choice was clear: Mum needed surgery or she would be in major chronic pain. She needed surgery to have any hope of walking again.

The surgeon left to begin his preparations, and they wheeled Mum away to prep her. I phoned Doug to fill him in and he said he'd relay the news to Jan. I can't remember whether I'd called Doug and Norma earlier or not. Possibly I'd waited until I had something definite to say; after all, they'd be at their cottage. This being Thanksgiving weekend, the whole family would be there. I didn't expect anyone to come keep me company, hadn't felt the need to ask for it either.

They did the surgery that night. Dick came up from Montreal the next morning, so I didn't go in, giving him space to do his doctorly thing, and form his own assessment of Mum. I went down to her old cottage by the river, now my grounding place. I brought beer and fixings for sandwiches, and Dick joined me there for a late lunch after he left the hospital. He reported that Mum seemed to have had a stroke at some point during or after the procedure. I told Dick about Friday's strange trip to the hospital. Perhaps she'd had a small stroke that day as well. This was possible, furthering Dick's belief that Mum's dementia was largely stroke related, not Alzheimer's. By now, for me at least, the classification was incidental, since the effects, and the results were much the same.

We fell silent, gazing out over the water, following the flight of a great blue heron gliding from one frog-hunting site close by to another one far down the bend in the river. Dick said that nature was taking its course, and that I shouldn't try to take on too much; helping Donald get back on his feet, learning to live with a disease that might jeopardize his ability to hold a steady job, was understandably more my priority now.

I told him what a privileged burden Mum had become. Then, looking at this habitually reserved, buttoned-down dear brother of mine, I laughed and told him that I'd come to think of myself as sucking at the teat of my mother, at long last. I saw the jolt go through him. Then he smiled, seeming to understand.

We'd finished the sandwiches and beer. Now we talked about the health-care directive. Dick said it was important that Mum's attending physician in the hospital have a copy and be on side. I said I'd bring in a copy and noted the name of the doctor who'd been assigned.

We looked out over the water some more. Dick wondered aloud whether Mum would be sent back to her old room at the residence or to a nursing home instead. It hadn't even occurred to me that she wouldn't go back to the residence. But then, I did-

n't yet know how serious the additional stroke Dick had reported
on had been, or I might have pursued it further. I said something
like, I assume back to the residence. Dick nodded as though in
agreement then got up.

After he left, I wandered back to the river's edge and sat back
down in what had become my own chosen lounge chair at
Mum's cottage. "Sucking at Mum's teat," I thought, and laughed
out loud at my having put it that way especially since I'd never
actually been suckled at my mother's breast. When I told Mum
I was getting married, she immediately said—literally, it was
almost the first thing out of her mouth, "Now, when you have
children, make sure you don't breastfeed or you'll lose your figure!" What that said about her estrangement from herself, I
thought now. From us, her children too. Then I remembered:
She wasn't fully present at our births either; wasn't conscious
even of her participation. She had chosen to be anaesthetized,
which was the fashion of the time, leaving it all to the doctors.

All those ruptures, breaks in the fabric of time! And then,
for me, the additional one of Mum having been ill for some time
after I was born. I have a vague memory of an Eastern European
nurse, Anna, who looked after Mum and us: a dress down almost
to her ankles, her hair up in a bun. I also remember kicking out
at her in a rage when Anna was trying to bathe me on the kitchen
table, in the white oval enamel laundry pan that went with
Mum's roller washing machine.

A kingfisher's shriek broke through my thoughts, and I
watched him swoop from his usual dead branch on the maple
tree by the river to drive another kingfisher away. The water was
calm, the motorboats moored for the night.

I sat on in the gathering twilight, and thought: There are
always ruptures and breaks: at birth, after birth; it keeps going on

and on. I was feeling this now not just with Mum, but with my beloved son whose illness had not only cut him off from his art but also, even with medication, sometimes affected his ability to think. What can one do with all these breaks and ruptures? There's no choice, really, except to go ahead and lean into the breaks, breathe into them in the everlasting longing for connection, and reconnection.

I didn't visit Mum at the hospital that evening. I knew that Doug was going; I'd leave him to it. So it was a shock when I went in on Monday: Mum had clearly slipped. She was asleep or dozing lightly, yet frowning every so often, moaning too, her mouth sagging open, hollow and empty because she didn't have her dentures in. Her right hand kept reaching down to her left leg, clutching at her thigh, trying, it seemed, to pull it up a little in the bed. She did this compulsively, again and again, without gaining whatever relief it was she was trying to achieve. I remembered Dick's mention of Mum having had another stroke. Was this it then? But this bad? Was this what he meant by nature taking its course?

The covers were in disarray, and the hospital shirt had pulled away from her side, exposing one breast. I moved a sheet to cover her. An abandoned hospital tray sat on a table on wheels beside the bed. There was tea in a mug that Mum hadn't drunk, some juice, and an untouched yogurt container. I pushed the table away so I could get to the cupboard to get Mum's cardigan to give her some warmth, and dignity too. But the clothes weren't hung up. They were in a clear plastic bag lying in the bottom of the cupboard. All the clothes she'd had on when she was brought in—what? less than two days ago—had been dumped into this bag then knotted at the top. Even her shoes and socks, maybe her undies too. I could see one shoe, its side pressed against the plastic, making it bulge. I stared at it, as though it was trying to tell me something, and I was too dense to get it.

I heard a noise, and closed the cupboard door. Mum was awake.

"Ah, there you are," she said as I came around the bed, a big smile on her face.

I leaned in to kiss her hello. I took her hand and fell to stroking her temple, smoothing back her hair like I'd done so many times over so many hours in the hospital on the Saturday. I suspect I did it to comfort myself too, after the shock of seeing my mother so drastically debilitated when I arrived. Yet, awake, Mum was positively chatty, beaming up at me. "You always seem to find me. How do you do it? " She asked, as though navigating the world was so far beyond her capacity to comprehend let alone manage herself that it had come to seem like magic. Her world had shrunk even further now, to little more than her body and her post-operative hip in the bed.

"It hurts, eh?" I asked as she kept pulling at her leg. By now I'd noticed that her left hand and arm hadn't moved since I'd arrived. The leg, I realized now, was affected too. When Dick had mentioned a stroke, I had assumed it had been as negligible in its effect as anything she'd suffered on the Friday or Saturday, while Dick, not having seen her either of those days to know what a difference this latest stroke had made, was unaware of my ignorance.

"Yes," Mum said. She frowned and looked at me hard. "Why does it hurt?"

Still holding her hand, still leaning in close, I explained as I had on Saturday, how she'd fallen and broken her hip, so they'd sent her to the hospital, where she had to have surgery. And then, I added, "You had a stroke."

Mum kept looking at me hard. "I might have another one."

The shock of this went through me like a shaft, both pain and light. That Mum had this much insight!

I held her gaze. "Yes, Mum, you might," I said.

If she was checking this out with me, she had her answer. It was okay with me. Barely.

Eventually, of course I suggested tea. From my own times in the hospital as well as hers, I knew enough to go looking for a kitchen with a kettle and stash of teabags and even, sometimes, cookies. While the water was heating, I found the nurse in charge of Mum this shift. I gave her the health-care directive I'd brought in for the doctor. She clipped it inside Mum's chart. I also told her that even though they had Mum's nametag over her bed accurate according to her health card, Elizabeth Anne Menzies, she answered to Anne, not Elizabeth. The nurse agreed to change it, and mentioned Mum's hearing aids. I said that they should have been with her things. Yes, the nurse said, but Mum didn't seem to like them in. Oh that, I said, and explained that this was a chronic problem; Mum often got fed up with the things in the residence too.

It took me a while to find a way to sit with Mum over tea. I couldn't risk lowering the bed rails, even if I could have found the correct lever or button at the end of the bed to do this. I ended up dragging the visitors' chair close in, plunking a pillow on the wooden arm, and perching myself there, leaning my shoulder against Mum's bed, close enough that we could touch each other often. I needed and wanted to do this. No matter if it comforted Mum, it comforted and grounded me.

We soon settled into a daily routine. While the doctors came and went, and a physiotherapist assessed Mum's needs in learning to walk again, plus her cognitive capacity for the therapy, we idled our time away with tea and visits, negotiating the chrome and hard edges around Mum's bed. I nodded to the other women in the ward, also recovering from hip surgery, and to the family members, middle-aged children like me, who came and went. Among them was a man who regularly visited the elderly woman in the bed opposite, probably his mum. She moaned and complained a lot, and constantly asked when she could go home.

He always sat in the visitor's chair several feet away from the bed, looking just as miserable as she did, and just as alone. His hands hung limp and useless between his knees as he sat there, offering up some little thing by way of conversation, then falling silent again when it went nowhere—perhaps because his mother was past that level of communication, and he didn't know this because he'd just arrived on the scene of his mother's decline, with a phone call about a fractured hip.

I wanted to go over to this man, a complete stranger. I wanted to take him by the hand, and close the distance between his mother's flesh and his own. I wanted to tell him: just touch her, hold her hand, stroke her face. Yes, she's strange lying there without regular clothes on, her hair a mess, her face so waxy and pale. But she's still there, inside all that strangeness. Reach in for her. Make contact skin to skin. Let yourself go, trusting the rhythms of gesture and pure relating.

I've since read some literature on "therapeutic touch" or "healing touch," and suspect that this is all part of it, though the model that's been developed by Dolores Krieger, a nurse specializing in neurophysiology, and Dora Kunz, a natural healer, doesn't involve actual touch at all. It operates on a premise that neuro-electric science is only now beginning to quantify: That we are embodied fields of energy immersed in larger fields of energy, and that the energy of individual bodies radiates beyond the skin, while the energy in others around us in turn permeates our being, and even connects us. Some call this "universal energy" or "the energy of creation," while others, who approach therapeutic touch as a spiritual practice, call it "sacred energy." In their article "An Overview of Therapeutic Touch and its Application to Patients with Alzheimer's Disease" for the July/August 1998 issue of the *American Journal of Alzheimer's Disease and Other Dementias*, nurses Randy Griffin and Evelyn Vitro report optimistically on the technique's success on people with severe and advanced dementia, mitigating agitation and confusion and relieving anxiety. They describe it as a "universal life energy that supports all living organisms and through which all matter and consciousness are interconnected." In China, the article continues, this energy is called "chi." In India, it's called "prana" and linked to breathing, with exercises called "paranayana" used to balance life-energy flow.

People trained in healing touch learn to centre themselves, entering almost a meditative state of attentiveness in which they can sense a breach in someone's energy flow by running their hands along the body inches above it. Maureen Kellerman, who does healing touch part time at the church that I attend, uses the words "thick" and "spiky" to describe when she senses a disruption in the balance, a rupture in the flow which otherwise should feel smooth. She can sense "if it's closed or open." If closed, her job is to re-open it, to get the energy flowing in harmony once again. She does this by consciously sending energy flowing out of her hands into the troubled energy field of the person with whom she's working.

"You're listening with your hands," she said, "processing things that you're reading energetically. You're reading things that are unseen, that you can't measure."

I told Maureen about the tea rituals with Mum, our holding hands, the familiar gestures of connection repeated time after time.

"I'd say you were interacting energetically with her," she said, suggesting too that it was likely having a "therapeutic effect." Anyone can have this effect, she continued. "If you're grounded and calm, and not easily thrown off, you're more likely to have a therapeutic effect on someone else."

It makes me wonder whether, as therapeutic touch continues to become mainstream, and regularly taught to staff caring for people in nursing homes, if its basics could also be taught to caregiving family members. I think of that wretched man sitting opposite his wretched mother moaning in bed with her pain-wracked hip. I think of myself, of my brother, Doug. How by learning some healing-touch techniques we might have helped our mothers. How we might have helped ourselves.

I think that of all my siblings I took Doug the most for granted during this period, or just plain ignored him. Communication between us was often through messages. I'd leave updates on Mum that way, and sometimes things I wanted to ask him. He too would leave a message on my phone: "Heather, this is Doug. Call me." His living in Ottawa was a convenient excuse too. Because he got to see Mum regularly, I could just assume he was picking up the same impressions as I was as she started to go downhill in the autumn; I didn't have to make any special effort to stay in touch, like I did with Janet and Dick. I did call him when I left the hospital that Monday after seeing the effects of the post-surgery stroke. I wish now that I'd gone in person, wish I could have arrived saying: "I need a hug." Instead, I gave him a call, and instead of voice mail, I actually got him live on the line. I asked him how he'd found Mum when he saw her on Sunday. "Pretty unresponsive," he said. He'd gone with the boys; they hadn't stayed long. Oh, I said. He didn't ask me how I'd found her. I didn't volunteer anything, and soon we said goodbye.

I went to Mum's residence to fetch her slippers and her favourite red velour dressing gown. I wound up her wall clock. I watered the plants on her windowsill. Then I sat in the cushioned chair normally meant for visitors and stared across at Mum's neatly made-up empty bed. Tears came, and I let them come, hugging Mum's dressing gown hard to my chest.

One day Mum would seem better, another day, worse. The hospital routines went forward, and I adjusted to them. The physiotherapist tried to teach Mum some simple exercises to strengthen her left leg then told the nurse that Mum couldn't manage to repeat them on her own. By now, the nurses and aides had taken to strapping Mum into the commode because she was too weak and uncoordinated to hold herself up on her own. Mum was classified as a two-person transfer, meaning that she needed someone on either side of her, or front and back. They strapped a wide belt around her middle to get a firm hold should Mum's body give way despite her best efforts to do what was expected of her.

One day I arrived to find them at this, the commode locked into position beside the bed. They'd given her a laxative, the nurse told me, because Mum hadn't been moving her bowels. Now she sat on the commode beside the bed, panting slightly, leaning forward, letting the belt anchor her, and looking utterly lost. I pulled a chair in close, leaned my forehead against Mum's, and placed my hands on hers. We sat like that for a while, and suddenly there was a terrible stench. It was all I could do to stay where I was. Then Mum shifted, and I pulled back. There was a wan smile on her face, relief, and accomplishment, perhaps a bit of both. I left it to the nurse or nursing aide to clean Mum up and clear away the mess, then watched as two of them hoisted Mum off the chair.

One of them explained to Mum that they were going to swivel her now, so if she could just stand there for a sec. And she did it. "Load bearing" they called it, an essential prerequisite to being able to walk again.

I tried not to overburden this with meaning, since everything else seemed to be going downhill. Mum had taken to dragging her glasses off, and letting them fall wherever they would among the bedding. So eventually the nurses stopped putting them on in the morning, and she never seemed to notice their absence. Mum's upper dentures were bothering her more and more too, and so she'd tongue them loose, and again, let them fall wherever they might. And soon, the nurses left the dentures too in the metal drawer in her bedside table alongside the box of hearing aids.

I grew used to the new look. Or perhaps by then I could see past it, focusing on Mum's bright hazel eyes, while my hands sought out her skin, holding her hand, brushing her hair if she wanted. Bringing a hot cloth for her face. Whatever came to me as something to give comfort, to us both, because by then it seemed that everything was reciprocal.

She had another mini-stroke. I arrived the next day with Donald, who'd decided he wanted to see Granny, and immediately I sensed that there had been another dramatic shift. In my journal that night, I wrote: "Her eyes have lost their shine. They're like an old flashlight bulb, barely emitting light. It seems to be an effort for her to talk; her voice is gravelly. She seemed to be surfacing from beneath a fog, and stayed somewhat submerged in it the whole time we were there."

I'd brought some maple flavouring to spruce up the eggnogs and Ensures they were plying her with. I told her this, maple being her all-time favourite ice cream. She rallied a little at the word, though it could as easily have been my enticing tone of voice. For when I brought the straw up to her lips, she just left it there, sitting against her lower lip, the muscles that normally puckered in a flash, ready to suck, to kiss, to latch on to life, were flaccid and inert. Plus, her head kept slipping off to the left; she couldn't hold it up. Her eyes kept closing, her good right hand moved restlessly in search of her by-now clearly useless left leg.

I kissed Mum on the lips, and she responded, but weakly. Though when I said, "I love you, Mum," she answered fully: "I love you too."

The nurse came to say that the social worker, Gail Dawson, wanted to see me in her office. I asked Donald if he minded staying with his granny. No problem, he said, and I watched him go down on his haunches, a move that put his young and vibrant head parallel to Mum's own head lying pale and wan on the pillow. This way, he could talk almost directly into her ear; so smart, I thought as I left; so perceptive and caring still.

In addition to Gail, Joanne, the head of the nursing unit for the ward joined us in Gail's comfortably furnished, dimly lit office. They introduced themselves. I introduced myself, all very formal and subdued. Gail invited me to sit down. There was a box of Kleenex on the table in front of me. I looked at it, and felt afraid; yet I was also excited. Was this the final drama? If so, I was ready. There was also a treacherous thought, a feeling almost of relief. I'd held up pretty well so far, I thought. But for how much longer? I was getting tired, my nerves on edge. It was hard, so hard, and part of me wanted it to end. Before I ran out of whatever—patience, love, and energy.

I sat there hypervigilant as Gail the social worker asked Joanne, the head nurse. "Do you think she'll make it?"

I looked at Joanne. "I don't think she will," Joanne said.

The words crashed into me. Hinges and latches gave way. Door-like things flapped back and forth inside my chest. Yet all this stayed hidden beneath my skin. One of the women handed me the Kleenex box. I took one. Yes, there were tears coming down my face. But I was outwardly calm. I'd been raised that way, trained that way, understood or assumed that there was merit in remaining that way in moments like this.

Still, I noticed a tremble in my voice when I spoke. That's also because I was agreeing with them. All my instincts said that Mum was on her way out of this world, for her own reasons or for none at all.

The air in the room seemed to start moving again after I said this. For the women, perhaps it was the sign they'd been waiting for, the permission to talk freely. Gail broached the subject of "palliative care." As I wrote in my journal later: "We cracked open the subject, made the shift: three women in a small, dimly lit room."

Joanne explained that Mum's hemoglobin was down to eighty-six; she needed a transfusion. But was it worth it? The health-care directive hung unspoken in the air, and frankly Joanne was of the opinion that upping the pain medication to provide the comfort that is palliative care's priority was more important.

They showed me Mum's chart, and it was almost too much to bear, seeing her set down in categories of bodily function, all in negative terms. Everywhere I read, there were clear, emphatic ticks indicating TA or "total assistance" needed in everything from toileting to feeding to movement in and out of bed. Everything was in the negative, the deficit category except at the very bottom, in the category for mood and overall bearing.

"Good affect," someone had written in the comment section. I smiled at this. "That's nice," I said, and the tears came again.

Joanne said that everyone liked having Mum on the ward as a patient. She was a good patient. She never complained, was always polite and said thank you for every little thing they did for her. I nodded as all these lovely statements flowed through me. I was crying freely now. Ah, Mum. Whatever was happening, Mum wasn't fighting it, wasn't fighting it at all. Perhaps she was ready. If so, the health-care directive was there like an open door. As Carleton University chaplain Tom Sherwood once told me, "Technology can get in the way of death." In other words, death is a process with its own time and timing, known only to the person who's dying and, even there, not necessarily consciously.

The literature, I've since read, is revealing. Apparently, people often talk in metaphors, telling it slant: They dream and speak of looking for a map, or for tickets or keys; getting their things together, going on a journey, going home. The stories I've been told or have read in books like Maggie Callanan and Patricia Kelley's *Final Gifts: Understanding the Special awareness, Needs and Communications of the Dying*, sometimes also include mention of people waiting on the other side, dying people seeming to see and hear someone or something beyond the reach of others' senses. All of this helps show, they say, "that dying people do have power."

Dr. David Kuhl, in his book *What Dying People Want: Practical Wisdom for the End of Life*, draws a useful distinction between knowing about dying and "knowing dying," and suggests that to fully live the process of dying involves a "transition from an outward journey to an inward journey." Part of this journey inward, he says, involves a life review, a final summing up, and reckoning. In his long practice in palliative care, he writes, he's watched people go about this, achieving serenity and peace in the process.

The most I knew of this myself at the time was when my then-oldest friend, Irene Spry, was dying at the age of ninety-one at home, under the patient care of her daughter, Lib. Lib and I had become friends over the years too, and I spent time with them both when I stopped by to visit. One evening, Lib told me of having told her mother that day: it's okay; you can let go. The literature on dying addresses this point: the importance of giving our loved ones permission to die. Still with her eyes closed, still in an almost comatose state, Irene replied: "Almost there." She died a day or two later.

But Irene had remained largely lucid, with her mind intact, virtually till the end, whereas Mum had little to go on, I thought. Still, I felt, believed or simply hoped, that at some level, Mum was still in the driver's seat of her life even now. Given what happened later, I think that she was.

Meanwhile, when I got back to the ward, Donald had pulled up a chair and was sitting more comfortably. He reported that Mum had been calling for me, even by name. I leaned in, saying hello. She opened her eyes and I told her I'd brought in some scissors. Her hair had been bothering her, I'd noticed, long enough by now that it was falling into her eyes. I got the scissors out of my bag, and showed them to her.

"Oh good," she said, and her inner being sat up straight and ready. I cranked up her bed, positioned more pillows to keep her propped up nicely, then set to work. Donald quietly positioned himself at my side, his hand out to receive each bit of hair as I cut it off with the scissors.

"Can I have some of her hair?" he asked. Sure, why not? So he pocketed each strand as I cut it off, first at the top, and then on either side. He stood patiently beside me, going even quieter as I grew still myself. I took my time, combing out Mum's hair, sectioning another bit for cutting, running the strands gently through my hands, clamping my fingers to hold it, memorizing it against my skin, then, snip, and handing it over to my son.

Mum opened her eyes when I'd finished, and smiled almost brightly

"That's better," she said.

Donald indicated the lunch that had been brought in on a tray and left on the bed-table when I was down the hall meeting with Gail and Joanne. Clearly Mum wasn't interested in the sandwich, so Donald wolfed it down. He indicated the mug, filled with by-then lukewarm tea.

"Tea," I said to Mum in a cheery, hortatory voice. I added some milk then held the straw up to Mum's mouth. She left the straw sitting there against her lower lip then turned her head away. I called her back, though inwardly thinking, why bother? Eventually she swallowed a single mouthful.

"Enough," she whispered, turning away again and closing her eyes as well.

I stroked her forehead. I pulled up the red dressing gown for extra warmth.

"Sleep well," I said, leaning forward to kiss her on the mouth, aware of the possibility that this might be goodbye. I felt a faint tightening of her lips against mine in response, and then we left.

We were quiet in the car as I drove Donald back to his place. Then he told me that when he'd been at Mum's bedside he'd told his granny that he loved her and she'd replied: "I love you too." Then she added, still looking at him hard: "Remember that."

Really? That he would say that to his granny! That Mum would say what she did in return. I looked over at my dear, lovely sensitive son. I think he understood that he'd just been blessed.

8

Finding a Nursing Home

The season had definitely turned. The fall rains had begun, bringing the leaves soggily down from the trees. The swallows had long since flown south, leaving the robins and sparrows; but they, anticipating winter, were essentially silent. Only the geese called out, high and urgent in the grey-flannelled sky, in a language no human can understand.

Mum didn't just fade away and die that week. Her vital signs indicated that she'd "stabilized," though at such a low level of function that she was barely there. It was like she'd gotten snagged on a branch nearly at the bottom of a cliff. She wasn't coming back up; there was no hope of that. But she wasn't dying either.

Now what? They wanted to discharge her, preferably to a nursing home. I drew a big, ragged breath, trying to get my bearings in the world beyond Mum's hospital ward, including the rest of the family. Jan on the phone from Edmonton was in favour of Mum going back to her room at the seniors' residence to see if she could make it or, left unspoken, be allowed to die in familiar surroundings. Dick, on the phone from Montreal, had much the same thoughts. Doug had no opinion one way or the other. But the nurses at the hospital certainly did. They even hinted to me that we were deluding ourselves to even consider anything other than a nursing home. And deep down, I agreed. I was read-ing something different from what the vital signs had to say, to doctors like Dick. I'd written in my journal only a day or two ago: "She's shrivelled away so much! Like a fire that's sputtering; throwing no heat anymore, and barely any light."

I'd found Mum not in her room, but in an alcove at the end of the hallway that day, with others in geriatric chairs. These are essentially recliners on wheels, though smaller and with more padding on the sides. They had propped Mum up in one of these, with extra pillows to keep her from sliding sideways, and another to hold her head as upright as possible. Her red velour dressing gown was on top of the hospital blanket, the one touch of colour, even of life it seemed, on the scene.

A nursing aide was feeding Mum lunch when I showed up. She moved to let me take over, but I said no, carry on. I was repelled by what I saw. Because Mum's eyes were closed, it looked like forced feeding, and it made me angry. Mum's closed eyes were saying that she really didn't want to be at the table, and this was her only way of showing it without making a fuss. She opened her mouth to receive the spoonful of mushed-up meat and potatoes whenever the aide tapped the spoon against Mum's lip, but her face remained totally slack and her eyes com-pletely shut. Mum wasn't taking any interest in the food; she seemed to be beyond that now. I watched the nursing aide fin-ish feeding Mum her lunch, going at it with dogged, patient efficiency. "Just shovelling the stuff into her mouth, and Mum keeping her eyes closed the whole time," I wrote later, adding: "It occurs to me that we are becoming more and more irrelevant as she slips away."

Partly, I wanted her to slip away: I was sure Mum wanted to as well. She didn't need or want food in her mouth and stomach weighing her down. But who was I to say it was time? Who was I to know anything? Meanwhile, I learned later, the code of ethics is clear: If a patient is willing to receive food when it is presented on a spoon or fork, hospital staff are duty bound to keep providing it.

Later that same day, when I bent close, holding Mum's good right hand, and said "I love you very much," she opened her eyes briefly, smiled up at me and said, "I love you too." A few moments later, she even repeated the whole statement: "I love you very much." She kept her eyes closed, but she squeezed my hand every so often, and I squeezed back, an ongoing beat of connection, skin-to-skin contact with all the feeling this evoked and released! She was still feeding off this, and so was I.

Now I had to face outward: to learn about nursing homes and waiting lists, to go out and find one with a bed available, or negotiate getting Mum back to her old room at River Park Place. I also had to work all this out with Doug, with Jan, and with Dick, to find the right words to chart the right path for everyone. I had no confidence that I could simply speak my truth, share the impressions I was confiding to my journal. Instead, I put on my Menzies-family armour, resolving to perform well and not be weak. I could do this thing; I could!

I made an appointment to meet with the director of care at the seniors' residence to see about getting Mum moved back there. If Jan and Dick wanted her there, I'd do my best to please them, if nothing else. I also wanted to leave no stone unturned, to be above reproach, though who would reproach me I couldn't have said. I walked briskly through the main entrance to the residence, though I noticed a turgid heaviness in my legs. It got worse as I was ushered into the boardroom and saw the director of care Deanna, the head nurse Sandi, and another nurse who looked after medications. The sight of them filled me with dread. I took a deep breath, sat down, and brought out my notebook with the points I'd recorded when talking with the hospital staff about the level of care that Mum needed. At my request, they'd also given me a copy of Mum's chart for the past few days. I wanted to be honest and above board, and so I'd come prepared to show Deanna and her staff everything. In return, I expected them to meet me half way. I especially looked to Sandi, a cheerful, no-problem kind of woman who liked Mum a lot, I knew, and with whom I'd always gotten along well.

I gave them time to read through all the charts, although each told the same brutal story in its grid of functions from "mobility" to "personal care" to "eating," "communication," and "daily living" down the side, then a list of gradients across the top indicating level of function from "independent" to "needs cueing/supervision" to "needs assistance" to "total care." Almost without exception, the ticks were still all on the far right side of the chart, clearly and unequivocally indicating "total care" required—even, still, for bladder and bowel. The commode was required on a regular basis.

The comments were daunting too. In the first box, under "tolerance" and "stamina," someone had written one word: "None." Under Mobility, someone had written, "Needs positioning." Under personal care, "Needs support in bath. Chair? Mechanical lift?"

The three women spent so little time looking at the charts it was as though they already knew what was on them, as though they'd already been in touch with the hospital. They had "concerns," they said, and started in on them. I duly began writing them down, being competent and conscientious, because their resistance was phrased so reasonably, as merely the issues I'd have to systematically address before they'd take Mum back.

I'd have to arrange for extra nurses so Mum could have twenty-four-hour care, they said. Okay, I said, writing this down. But, these agency people are totally unreliable, they said. "People don't show up," one said. "And then we'll be calling you," another added. Then, Deanna the director of care added: "You'll be putting Mum at risk."

Had they rehearsed this? I looked from one to another. Not a hint of doubt, no crack at all in their united front against me. At least that's how it felt. I turned to Sandi and asked what she felt about Mum coming back.

"She's too heavy a load. Definitely too heavy," Sandi replied.

It was as though this load Sandi spoke of was coming down on me, like bricks sliding off a board onto my shoulders and back. I was speechless, numb. Sandi's gaze was unflinching; I turned away, determined not to cry or admit defeat. Then they turned strategic. If Mum came back to the residence, she'd be off the priority list for placement in a nursing home should she need one after all, one of them said.

Deanna added: "You'll be making a lot of changes that may not be necessary."

I looked at her, the phrase "may not be necessary" caught in the space between my ears, like a knot that cannot be untied. What did she mean by "necessary"? Necessary for whom? In terms of what? I knew that Deanna was saying something important, but I couldn't grasp it, couldn't hear the implied end to the sentence: necessary in the *end*. I wasn't trying to deflect and avoid the truth. As far as I knew, I was trying really hard to face up to it. I felt like shouting, like crying.

After the meeting, I went to Mum's old room to find her memory book. I had a vague idea that getting Mum to look at it would help me get clear on where she should be, give me something concrete to relay to my siblings. I got into the car, put the key in the ignition and noticed that my arms felt heavy, even tingling slightly, which was odd. What time was it? Late in the day. I'd set myself up coming alone. Three against one. I should have called Norma to come with me. Plus, I'd been dumb. I hadn't paced myself. I'd come to this meeting straight from the hospital and a telephone conversation with the doctor who hadn't exactly been encouraging either. Yes, he'd told me, Mum's vital signs were showing physical improvement. "But mentally, she's quite deteriorated," he said. He allowed that she was "sometimes alert," but "only minimally alert," he added. I wrote all this down, as though I was a news reporter collecting the facts, just the facts. Yet the doctor had ended by saying essentially, why not? Mum might still benefit from being back in her old familiar surroundings. "It's hard to say; you never know. Though definitely," he told me, "she definitely needs a nursing-home level of care."

I have no memory of getting myself out of the River Park Place parking lot, nor where I went next. Probably back to my apartment to collect the dog, and take her out for a walk. I was feeling too lonely and alone by then to phone a friend, reaching out to be held. Somehow, though, I ended up back at the hospital, ostensibly to show Mum the memory book.

I kissed her hello, and felt her smile like a warm cloth against my face. I don't think I even asked if she wanted tea, just went off to the kitchen to make some for us both. I pulled up the visitor's chair, plunked the pillow on the arm, and took up my now-familiar perch where I could hold Mum's good hand in mine and drink my tea with the other. I reported on my meeting with the people at River Park Place, relayed the greetings they'd asked me to convey. Mum smiled throughout all this, but showed no real sign of comprehension. I asked her if she liked the view out her window. She frowned as though she didn't understand what this meant. I opened up the memory book, to the early pages showing her original home in Sherbrooke, her beloved father, her favourite dog, and of course herself. Nothing. I pulled out the photo I'd taken at the residence a year or so ago, showing Mum sitting on her bed, her dog Coffee on the floor beside her.

"That's you in the residence," I said.

"Oh yes," Mum said vaguely, but showing no real interest and zero recognition. Her eyes kept closing, her head listing off to the left. A nurse came by to check on Mum, and asked to look at the photos.

"Such a gracious woman," the nurse said like so many of the others had said. And "such a lovely smile." I nodded, tears welling. The nurse touched my arm briefly, and left.

I put the photos and memory book aside, and just sat there holding Mum's hand. When she opened her eyes again, I returned to my question, this time simply asking: "Do you want to go home?"

She looked at me puzzled. "I don't know," she said, her eyes on mine.

I tried something simpler still. "Are you happy here?"

"Yes," she said emphatically. I squeezed her hand. She squeezed mine back. Then she closed her eyes again, and drifted away into the doze she spent more and more of her time suspended in. I came away feeling certain that it didn't really matter where Mum was, as long as she was warm and dry between the sheets, and someone like me popped in every so often to hold her hand, to smile, and repeat those primal phrases: "Hello, it's me," "I love you," and "I love you very much," to steady her; that's all.

When I got home I wrote in my journal: "It seems to me that Mum is adrift in a sort of dream state, a sort of amniotic sea of impressions, feelings. I imagine them as diffuse, not tied to specific memories, just sensations. Warm nutrients of a sort, but less to do with building up. More an un-building. Just letting it all slip away."

If only I'd started with that when I got on the phone to my siblings: just being myself, alive to what I was sensing, confiding in them what I was recording in my journal. If only I'd been true to how exhausted I was by then, not up to being in the driver's seat on this at all. But I couldn't. The family culture, steeped in mind-over-matter, stiff upper lip and self-control, was too strong in us all, myself included. Nor could I risk having them think: Poor thing. She's not up to the challenge, getting on with the job, not tough enough when it comes to the crunch. Someone else will have to take over—Janet most likely. She had talked of coming east in a week or so.

We didn't grow up close as children. Partly, because everything revolved around Mum, pleasing her, appeasing her, vying for her attention and approval by doing her bidding or, even better, anticipating it. Equally, the force field drove each of us at least a bit into our own separate version of removal: Janet with her horse that she trained in dressage and showed at the local fall fair, me in my solitary rambles, though sometimes too with Doug, who was a rambler too, while Dick stayed close to home with Mum until he was sent to a private school four hours' drive away at the age of twelve or thirteen. Actually, Dick and I were close when he was young, until he was sent away to school though we had gradually renewed our closeness as adults. Jan and I too grew closer as adults: first spending a summer youth hostelling around Europe and later, buying a house together in Edmonton, before I moved back east in my late twenties. Doug and I were quite close for a few years too, particularly as he clashed more and more with Mum, and I became his shoulder to cry on. Once, when I was thirteen or so and he, sixteen, he did literally cry on my shoulder, after Mum had got so angry at some stupid thing he'd done, playing hooky I think it was, that she actually said: "I wash my hands of you," turned her back on him, and went outside to the garden.

But over the years, I grew tired of having to defend myself for defending Mum to Doug, tired too of how he seemed to hoard his anger and resentment toward her, relishing in calling her "my enemy." By the time of Mum's decline, Doug and I had less and less to say to each other. In fact, when I visited, he often kept on with whatever he was doing: pacing in the next room while muttering case notes into his Dictaphone or, outside, mulching the ground under his gorgeous dahlias, re-potting some forlorn houseplant he'd brought home from the office, leaving Norma and me to our tea, or glasses of wine, talking about our kids, our mothers, our work, the books we were reading, and the issues of the day.

I'd often worried that when something came up and we children would have to pull together, the four of us wouldn't come together well. Now here it was Friday night, the end of a long workweek for most of us, and I for one was flattened with fatigue. The sensible thing would have been to wait until the morning. Instead, I sat down at my work table, mind over matter, resolved to get on with it. I would do this thing: Serve as the family messenger, mediating the options and opinions, or at least clarify them before Jan arrived.

I spread all the "evidence" out in front of me: Not just what the doctor, nurses, and residence staff had told me, but the hospital's discharge policy, which spells out the hospital's right to move a geriatric patient to any nursing home with a bed available if none of the homes the family has chosen have one first, though the hospital will give you twenty-four hours' notice. I re-read the patient charts, with their "TC" shorthand for "total care required" in everything Mum used to do so blithely and matter-of-factly for herself.

On a separate sheet of paper, I jotted down some talking points, beginning with the status quo: "Daunting," I wrote. Not "I feel daunted," just "daunting," and underlined it twice. This was as far as I let my emotions into the picture: a double line under a gerund, a word rendered as its own self-sufficient action. I wanted to steer my siblings toward the idea that things were decidedly not good, and that a nursing home was probably the most sensible choice for Mum in the end. In fact, I also wrote down: "No longer so confident it's appropriate to go back to River Park," though without a pronoun indicating that it was I who dared to suggest this! Jan would see for herself when she got here, but meanwhile, she had the least sense of what was going on with Mum from day to day. I wanted to convey this as best I could, in language she would hear and heed. I transcribed some of the key quotes from the doctor, and from the staff at River Park Place, including "too heavy a load" and "wary" about having Mum back at the residence. I would suggest a two-pronged approach to everyone on the phone tonight: researching the availability of agency nurses to care for Mum back at the residence, and checking out local nursing homes with available beds. We could make a final decision once all this information was in hand.

I phoned Dick first, as a sort of dress rehearsal before a friendly audience. Then I phoned Jan, and went through what, by now, was a comfortable spiel, the facts spread out, the subjective stuff supported by quotes from the professionals. I have no record of Jan's and my conversation that night, only a vague recollection of being glad that she supported the two-pronged approach. Then, suddenly, she was talking about coming east in December, not right away. She'd been on the phone with Dick who had explained about Mum having stabilized then on the phone with Doug who'd suggested Christmas as a family.

Hearing her say this, something inside me gave way, the prospect of all that lay ahead was suddenly too much. Inwardly, I clamped down, fighting for control. And when I spoke again, I said only: "You might want to get flight insurance."

"Why?" she asked.

"In case you have to change your flight," I said. I left it at that in part because I was hurt that she still looked so much to Dick for information. She'd even started repeating what Dick had told her about Mum's vital signs over the phone, as though to set me straight on my own seemingly too-negative assessment. I held the phone away from my ear as if to flee the pain I felt, my sense of disconnect and thwarted communication. And I said nothing, just listened in silence as my older sister explained that she'd found a seat-sale for her flight and this way, she could drive down to Arizona and get herself settled for the winter before coming East. I continued to hold the phone slightly away from my ear, hearing the words go by but not fully taking them in, not even trying to hear, let alone acknowledge, the anxiety that might have been running beneath her chatter. I replied in kind, something about letting me know her flight plans, and left it at that, not offering a hint that I might need my sister right *now*.

I didn't say this too because I didn't trust that I could stay grounded in myself in her presence. Worse, I could set up defection in a second, in some anticipatory gesture of concession so fast and subtle neither of us would even notice. I had been doing it right there on the phone, muting myself, removing myself. Yet I had formed this lovely intimacy with Mum, each of us grounded in our feelings, speaking from our feelings of what was real to us in the moment, and I didn't want to risk losing it. And so, rather than going on faith that Jan could find her way into that same intimacy too, I turned away, conspired in keeping her away. I didn't want to chance being muted with Mum, not now. So I left it at that, betraying Jan by holding out on the truth that I was feeling at the time: that Mum was less and less in the land of the living, more and more... I couldn't put it into words, only feel it. Yet I felt it as surely as water being soaked up into the ground, the law of gravity ineluctably at work. Mum was more and more submerged, going with that flow and away. Her time left with us was probably days and weeks rather than months.

As I hung up the phone with Jan, there was another thought in my mind as well: my sister-in-law Norma, Doug's wife. Norma was my ace in the hole, the card up my sleeve. She was emotional like me; in fact, she brought out that side of me. Norma and I would look at nursing homes together. I'd go through the motions of seeking Doug's help, and he'd be happy enough to leave the work to us. With luck, I'd even get Norma on the phone and we'd take it from there.

Doug answered the phone. I asked him how he was, and told him I was fine too—"a bit tired, that's all," Ha! Then I got on with my by-now well-rehearsed talking points, ending with the proposal that we pursue a two-pronged approach, River Park Place or the nicest nursing home we could find. I paused, ready to hear his response, even with my pencil poised to take notes for future reference.

I didn't have to wait; Doug spoke immediately. "The state she's in, she might as well be in a kennel."

It was like the strap descending, the shadow of the strap coiled tightly on the shelf. I pushed the coiled phone cord away from my arm. I said something inane, just moving my lips really, to mitigate the moment. I don't even know what I felt in that instant, I moved so quickly to get beyond it. I ploughed on, into the practicalities of what needed to be checked out on both trajectories. I ended by asking for help but in a voice so straight-laced it was a matter-of-fact statement, not a personal plea.

"I need help on this," I said. Fair enough, Doug said, matching my tone, and notching it higher with brisk dispatch. He'd be willing to hire someone to take this on as a job, as a file. I tried for a wry chuckle, and suggested that something more personal might be appropriate, edging my way toward enlisting Norma's help. I asked if Norma was home; I'd like to speak to her.

No, Doug said. Norma had lost her mother only the previous year, and Mum being in the hospital was bringing back painful memories. "I want to insulate Norma as much as possible," he told me. Again, I tried to lighten things up with a laugh, and said that Norma and I were friends; she could speak for herself. So could I speak with her?

"No," he said. "She is my wife. I forbid you to talk to my wife."

"Oh?" I said, reeling.

"For as long as this goes on," he said.

"Forbid?" I queried back, still trying to lighten things up.

"I forbid you," he repeated, and then he hung up.

My hand was trembling as I put down the phone. Silence in my apartment, even the dog oblivious as she snoozed on the rug. Silence and more silence. I was utterly cut off and alone. I poured myself a scotch and stared at the curtain opposite me. I got up and went out onto the balcony, contemplated the sharp vertical drop. There'd been another moment when it had tugged at me like the perfect harmony line, but not tonight. I came back inside, closed the sliding door, pulled the curtains back in place, and poured myself another scotch, anticipating a headache in the morning. The weekend passed in a blur, although on Sunday I managed to prepare my class notes ready to teach my usual fall university course the next day. I also called Gail, who works part time as my research assistant and, adopting Doug's idea as my own, I hired her to look into nursing agencies. The social worker at the hospital had given me the list of nursing homes with beds available, and after marking some as possible candidates, I turned over the list to Gail as well. By the time I'd finished teaching on Monday, she hoped to have appointments for me to tour five nursing homes on Tuesday, plus some background on what twenty-four-hour nursing care was available part time.

By mid-afternoon on Sunday, I had everything lined up. I headed to the hospital to visit Mum. She was in her bed dozing when I arrived, and revived only briefly when I slipped my hand into hers, leaned over and whispered hello into her ear. She wasn't even interested in the tea I offered, letting the straw just sit there on her lower lip till I took the mug away. I cut her fingernails instead, marvelling at how much paler and thinner her fingers had become. I didn't feel much like talking myself, but didn't want to leave yet either. So I took the lotion from the bedside table, and massaged some of it into Mum's hands. She smiled as I did this.

"Lovely," she said, opening her eyes and looking deeply into mine. Tears welled up. I squeezed Mum's hands, and she squeezed back. I applied more lotion, and continued the circular motion round and round the familiar contours of Mum's hands, massaging my skin against hers, going with the flow of the motion, and it occurs to me now that a massage can serve as a medium of communication too. In fact, Marshall McLuhan suggested this himself when he once rephrased his famous aphorism, "the medium is the message" as "the medium is the *massage*," its effects are that visceral.

Mum's and my communication had settled into something this basic and primal: a meditation in hands, a medium of pure connection, a massage of energy across the skin, the largest of all the sensory organs, giving and receiving comfort if nothing else. It felt too as though the two levels of perceiving—the material and immaterial, the tangible and intangible, the conscious and the intuitive, had drifted together, bringing us into a realm that could be called spiritual.

I call it spiritual in the broadest possible sense, as shared breath and breathing and, with this, awareness at that fundamental level. In *Praying our Good*byes, Joyce Rupp describes this level as being "inside the heart of the experience." In the fourteenth-century classic, *The Cloud of Unknowing*, St. John of the Cross describes the spiritual as "the work of the inner life." In *I and Thou*, Jewish theologian Martin Buber suggests that we achieve the spiritual when we're so immersed in giving to and relating to the other (thou) that we lose a sense of the border between ourselves and that other being, and we merge with the larger Thou of God. He writes that "Man lives in the spirit . . . when he enters into this relation with his whole being." In his eloquent 1998 CBC Radio Massey Lecture *Becoming Human*, Jean Vanier, founder of the l'Arche network of communities for people with intellectual disabilities, defines this spiritual journey as "a movement of the heart . . . toward connectedness."

A common element in all this is the quality, depth, and integrity of relating to another, a willingness to be so fully present, so fully given over to relating that normal boundaries of space and time dissolve.

I cannot know what it was like for Mum, only for me, and the subterranean, unconscious journey I was engaged in as I sat as close as I could get to Mum in her hospital bed that November afternoon rubbing lotion into her hands. Consciously, in that moment, it was enough for me to simply be with Mum, drawing comfort and steadiness from that simple rhythmic motion. I grew calm, almost serene, as I sat there, moving my fingers across and around her familiar fingers, caressing the delicate skin around her wrists, hearing Mum sigh every so often, sighing myself as well. I wasn't conscious of being in a spiritual realm, but I was in a realm that was both inwardly deep and outwardly expansive. I was immersed in it, flowing with it: a realm of rhythm in motion lubricated by hospital-issue hand lotion. It was a realm in which Mum and I could relate to each other beyond the need or even the desire for words, could communicate our aliveness to each other, our eternal connection.

As I left and was walking down the hall, I recognized Doug at the far end coming toward me. My heart speeded up, my throat went dry. What would we say to each other? My mind was a blank. I stopped in a spot where there were no carts in the way, stepping into the extra space and giving Doug a chance to draw close. He was dressed in grubby gardening clothes; a pair of green boots on his feet, a patch of duct tape over one toe. He was carrying a clay gardening pot, and I could see a small plant sticking up in the middle. He carried the pot in front of him, in both hands, arms slightly extended away from his body, as though he was carrying an offering toward an altar. He walked resolutely, deliberately, the heel of his boots coming down firmly on the floor under him, his head erect, his eyes fixed forward on the distance he was covering to reach his mother.

"Heather," he said as he came within talking distance of me, his tone a honed mix of challenge, query, and acknowledgement that had, by now, become familiar as his habitual salutation. I'd grown used to the loneliness it evoked in me as well. I nodded, waiting until he would stop and look at me, my signal to speak myself. But he kept walking, his eyes never connecting with mine, and I watched his slightly hunched back, his oversized boots plunked down one after another as he walked the rest of the length of the hall, turned left, and disappeared into Mum's room, never glancing back once. I turned, and continued on my way toward the exit, though I stopped at the pay telephone downstairs and dialled his number, hoping to catch Norma at home, alone. She answered and I briefly explained my dilemma, that Doug didn't want me bothering her at this time. We agreed that we should respect Doug's feelings, said some words of comfort to each other and then goodbye.

Compared to family stuff, checking out nursing homes was a cinch. They all followed pretty standard procedures and standard staffing practices as well. Still, I made a point of asking, as Gail had cued me to do: What was the ratio of registered nurses (RNS) to nursing assistants versus aides? Aides have little medical training, mostly practical stuff like how to change linens and help to turn patients. Another key question: What was the staff ratio and competence level breakdown at night, and on weekends? As for their policy on sedatives and tranquilizers—sometimes called "chemical restraints"—the pendulum seems to have swung away from facile sedation, at least in the answers I got to my questions.

I wrote careful notes, constantly juggling each place into an internal ranking order. Dick would come up from Montreal on Saturday, and we'd view a short list of three before making a final selection. By now, the family consensus seemed to be leaning toward a nursing home for Mum.

Some homes were brighter than others, some more cluttered with handicrafts and small, personal bits of memorabilia stuck on doors and walls. Some smelled of urine, some of strong disinfectant or whatever they use to keep such institutions germ free. In some, the people in charge were unctuous; in others, officious. I preferred a casual efficiency, where feelings weren't laid on but left to surface in a moment that seemed appropriate. The "bath" rooms bothered me the most. So large, so full of chrome apparatuses: a lift, a hoist, straps, and other devices that were beyond my comprehension. Still, they left me with the overwhelming knowledge that here people didn't have baths, they didn't get into baths. They were given baths, they were put into baths. There was no aesthetic relief. Other, more functional priorities took precedence. The large and engineered space made it clear: The bodies that entered here were largely inert, acted upon, not acting of their own volition. Mum would be one such body on their list. So I made a point of paying attention to details in the "bath" room, ranking ones with the most supportive technology ahead of others, though the sight of them depressed me the most.

I also noticed the patients: many of them still beneath their layers of clothes, dressing gowns, and blankets. Some of them bulged in unexpected places. Most of them were gaunt and pale. Heads drooped forward; eyes sometimes open, sometimes closed. Often, mouths sagged open, saliva meant for savouring good food and drink, sliding away from slack lips, wasted, and forgotten. But then I caught an unscripted moment when some staff person tucked a terrycloth bib under a saliva-soaked chin, and that's what I paid most attention to in the end: the empathy in the air, in the tone of voice, in a hand reaching out to touch, to tuck, to stroke. The social model of care as important as the medical model, if not more so here. A small nursing home, Orchard Lodge, seemed to have that quality of engagement more than others. I quietly made it my first choice, hoping that Dick would feel it too, and agree.

On the Wednesday, after my second day of nursing home tours I had to stop by the hospital anyway. They wanted to move Mum to the geriatric floor, where they keep patients awaiting transfer to nursing homes, and had asked me to remove some of her stuff. Still, some instinct also had me focused on Mum. I wanted to see her. I was tired. I had a headache. I needed my mummy, pure and simple. I had in mind that I would sing to her. I don't know why; only that almost from the moment of leaving the last nursing home, which had been one of the smelliest, with the most vacant-looking, abandoned-looking patients, I was remembering some of the songs Mum had taught us during car rides to and from the farm all the weekends of my childhood. As I drove to the hospital, I found myself rehearsing them even, knowing that this was what I would do, for her, for me, and wanting the words ready when the moment came to call on them.

She wasn't in her bed when I arrived, so I went looking for her at the end of the hall where patients in geri chairs were usually parked. Sure enough, Mum was in the alcove at the end of the hall, propped up in a geri chair, an abandoned food tray on the table beside her. She had white socks on her feet that came up over her knees; for warmth, the nursing aide had told me because Mum in her restlessness would often pull the covers off herself, and the socks at least kept her feet from getting chilled before someone came along and covered Mum up again. I re-arranged the covers around her, along with Mum's red dressing gown, which had become a permanent part of her world. When she roused at my presence, I propped an extra pillow under her head to help hold it up. Then I pulled the visitors' chair close and, sitting on the arm, leaned into the space where Mum lay back in the geri chair. I held her good hand in both of mine and began with "Love's Old Sweet Song," a bittersweet favourite of hers: "Just a song at twilight, turn the lights down low. As the flicker-ing shadows, softly come and go." I stumbled over words like "flickering shadows" as the words suddenly turned on me, tak-ing on a whole new meaning. Still, I kept going, my voice wob-bling a bit, my eyes firmly locked on Mum's eyes which, suddenly bright with tears, held me up as I sang clear through to the end.

Mum squeezed my hand. "Lovely," she said, her voice a joy-ful whisper. "Lovely, Heath, lovely," she said when I'd finished.

"Clementine?" I asked, switching to something a little lighter. It was an old favourite of Mum's on which she used to improvise her own harmony line. Again, the smiling face, the eyes gleaming with life, the hand squeezing mine and, "Lovely" whispered as a recurring refrain. My bum was getting sore sitting on the edge of the chair, and my back ached from the extreme bending. But I wanted to go on and on. I was drawing Mum out, I could tell, and the beloved songs, though nominally forgotten, were doing the pulling. As Sacks writes from his experience with using music as therapy for people with dementia, "Music ... can orient and anchor a patient when almost nothing else can." It can also anchor and orient the caregiving family members, people like me, I think now.

"There is still a self to be called upon," Sacks continues, "even if music, and only music, can do the calling."

At the time, I had one other thing in mind as I sang Mum into the realm of these still-familiar songs. I wanted somehow to broach the subject of death, give Mum a chance to speak of it, and any fears she might have. I'd approached the subject, obliquely, a few months ago, asking Mum if she believed that there'd be someone (I had Dad in mind) to greet her on "the other side." "No," she said. "I think you just die and that's the end." I waited for her to go on but she didn't. That seemed to be all she had to say on the subject. But maybe she'd say something now, look to me to say something. I had no idea.

Regardless, it felt good sitting there singing, leaning my forehead against Mum's across the space of the geri chair. It was as though she was feasting on these old, deeply familiar songs. Certainly I was; I could feel my headache easing. I chose another song, "Swing Low, Sweet Chariot," took a breath, and smelled the familiar scent of Mum's breath coming in through my nose, a faint after-taste of tea. Then I sang, in the low alto voice I have inherited from Mum, letting myself go down with those deep, low notes, and then up again with "Comin' for to carry me home." I hadn't rehearsed this song, and so, as I sang that line, the words caught me by surprise. I realized, suddenly, they might mean "Comin' for" my mother, to carry her "home."

I hovered there for a moment as the meaning hit me, hovered in the space before the next note, in the blank space where imagination enters, and then I was drawn forward, by the momentum of the song itself.

"Swing low," the song went on. My voice cracked as I went

on with it, pulled by the song's powerful rhythm, and my commitment to singing it for Mum. My throat ached and ached as the meaning of the words took hold of me, another "home" beyond my power to know, or to enter myself. I was wobbling into the next iteration of "comin' for to carry me home" when a voice cut in. It was Gail, the social worker. At first I couldn't make out what she was saying, she seemed to be talking so fast, or so softly that I couldn't make out the words: Something about power of attorney for personal care.

I was furious. How dare she interrupt? I told her to look in Mum's chart; she'd find all the necessary forms there. But she didn't go away. She stood there still, and I forced myself to pay attention. It was clear that there was a difference between power of attorney for medical care and for personal care. What the hell? What stupid bureaucrat thought this up?

No, I told Gail, there was nothing prepared. We hadn't realized there was something separate. She explained, probably with infinite patience but which I was in no mood to acknowledge let alone be soothed and cued by, that this power of attorney specifically dealt with placing someone in a nursing home or other institution if they were unable to make the decision themselves. She had the forms in her office, she said. All four children would have to sign them, though emailing instructions would be fine.

Fine, I said, following her to her office. I took the envelope she'd thoughtfully put everything into, then went back to Mum's room to pick up her stuff as I'd been asked to do. I opened the cupboard by the side of the bed, and there was the clear plastic bag filled with the clothes she had on the Saturday they'd brought her in here by ambulance, nearly a month ago: the pants, the shirt and sweater, the socks and the shoes Mum had been walking around in mere weeks ago. I looked at the bag, a bubble of time that had gotten caught in an eddy behind some rock in a stream, and would not burst. I grabbed the bulging bag and let it bang against my leg as I carried it away.

Somehow, I got through the rest of the week and was ready, notes in hand, when Dick showed up on Saturday morning. He arrived driving not the usual family van but a black Mustang convertible. It was a recent self-indulgence, he admitted, advancing middle age and all that. Sure I said, and readily agreed to using it, instead of my driving him around in my old Toyota. I slipped into the low-slung passenger seat, blinking at the November sunlight dancing off the shiny hood. He revved the motor into the traffic on Baseline, clearly enjoying the car's deft power, and showing it off to his sister. He looked tired and pale, like I was probably looking those days as well. And yet there was a jaunty energy about him. Possibly it was from the car, possibly too from the shift out of the ordinary that had caused him to step away from his family, for us both to be meeting alone, in a different context than usual. It infected me as well, and I began to relax.

Everything went as I'd set it up, with someone expecting us and ready to provide a quick tour as soon as we arrived. Dick took in details I had missed, knew things without having to be told. He asked the occasional question, but mostly seemed to feel informed enough with what I had told him, and what he could take in with his experienced doctor's eye. I had saved my first choice, Orchard Lodge, for the last, and he immediately agreed with me that this would suit Mum the best. So that was that. Now to the hospital, I said, where we could tell Mum together.

He didn't think that was necessary, yet I persisted. I wanted to get him in to see Mum again. Because of a sense I had? I don't know. I knew, or I could imagine, that it was hard for Dick to not have his mummy recognize him anymore. But I hoped he'd put up with that, and in we went.

Mum was propped up in bed, with the covers all in place, when we walked into the ward, and she opened her eyes at the sound of our voices saying hello. But it was clear that, sure enough, she didn't recognize her youngest son, her baby. Still, Dick took it well. There was a lunch tray sitting on the bedside table and Dick turned to it as though it was a prop set there precisely for this scene. I stood on the right side of the bed, holding Mum's good right hand while Dick moved in close on the left-hand side, the food tray positioned at his elbow. First he surveyed the food to select what would do Mum the most good, starting with cranberry juice. Gently, he placed the straw against Mum's lower lip and, when she opened her mouth a little, slipped it in. Silence as Mum sucked in some juice, swallowed, sucked in some more, swallowed again. I could sense Dick relaxing as though having had Mum receive something from his hands was recognition enough. She lapsed back into a half doze. I leaned in and started telling her about the nursing homes we'd visited. Mum opened her eyes and looked at me in the searching way I'd grown used to. By then I had come to believe that as words had lost their meaning, she relied more and more on body language, the steadiness of my gaze and the cadences of my voice, the basic alphabet of love. She heard at a level that I was unaware of, trust making up, perhaps, for cognition.

Gesturing to include Dick, I told her that the two of us had just picked a nursing home we hoped she'd like, and described the room a little, the view toward the river out the window, the bird feeder hanging from a tree nearby. They would move her there in the coming week, I told her. "Okay?"

She didn't say yes or no, although she nodded as though she'd taken in something of what I'd said. She glanced at Dick then back at me and smiled.

Dick surveyed the food on the tray: mashed up turnips, potatoes, some form of dark-brown meat, also mashed up, and gravy. Always gravy. Dick loaded up a spoonful and, telling Mum what was coming, carried it to her lips. Obligingly, she opened her mouth, and allowed Dick's spoonful of food to enter.

"That's nice," she whispered, looking at Dick briefly, and it was as though she was recognizing something after all: familiar facial gestures—some a lot like Dad's, plus familiar tones and rhythms in his voice. By now, too, Dick had become downright voluble, mostly on the subject of food and feeding. He was also calling her "Mum," not "Mother" as he'd fallen into the habit of doing over the years. I noted this shift in my journal later. To me at least, it meant that Dick had slipped through his own reserve and was fully here, whether Mum knew him by name or not. It was love talking through all that patter about what food he was loading onto the spoon, the careful positioning of the spoon by Mum's lips waiting for an opening, then slipping it in, love in those pale heaps of turnip, meat and potato, in the patient waiting. Deeply nourishing love. Mum smiled, her eyes bright; she was clearly enjoying herself.

I kissed Mum goodbye, told her I'd be back soon. Dick kissed her too, and then we were off. A lovely late, late lunch, and then, while Dick headed back to Montreal, I headed to the store for groceries, then back to the apartment to collect the dog. Next, I drove to the Baxter Conservation Area for a long and restoring walk. The sun was slipping behind the trees when we got there and as we walked along the boardwalk, the sky flared a bright crayon orange, then mellowed and faded against a deepening turquoise blue. For safety's sake it was time to turn back, for it had grown dark in the woods. I'd been attacked more than once in my life and had learned to respect my fears.

As I turned the corner where the path opens onto a meadow by the parking lot, the moon was suddenly right in front of me: a full moon, stained amber brown from the Earth's dust and dirt, cross-hatched by the treetops in the distance. I stood still and watched as the moon worked its way free of the obstructing trees, free of the Earth's lingering dust and finally floated, bone white and pure, up into the clear night sky.

9

Safe Passage

I was having strange dreams, wildly different in landscape, yet always the same. I was lost, or Mum was lost. I'm not sure which, only that I was looking for Mum. I was always looking for Mum, propelled by a terrible, tight anxiety as though it was my fault she was lost, and nobody else seemed to know how helpless she was on her own. In one dream, I dashed about behind ten-wheeler trucks in look-alike loading bays on the backside of a shopping mall. There were ambulances in between the trucks, and I went from one to the other asking if they had my mother. In another, I was in a building. Someone I recognized was saying it was time for me to give my speech, but I could hear what sounded like Mum's voice from the other side of a partition. I went around the screen, and saw the woman who was speaking. It seemed to be Mum alright. She had her hair up in that signature roll on top and on the side of her head. Yet it wasn't Mum; I just knew it. It was someone impersonating Mum, to put me off. In the dream, I said these words out loud: "It's someone impersonating Mum." I kept saying this to whomever it was who wanted to get on with introducing my speech. I was so angry. I stood behind the partition, listening avidly to what this woman was saying, pouncing finally on a phrase my mother would never ever use. See, I said to this man, proof that this was an impostor. And that was the end of the dream.

It didn't help that they kept moving Mum from one room to another on the geriatric ward, because they were re-wiring the rooms, and had to take the ceiling tiles down. I'd arrive to find the room empty, and had to find a nurse who could redirect me. On Sunday, Mum was at least in the same room as on Saturday when Dick and I had come together. This time, however, when I pulled aside the yellow curtain, I froze. Mum's eyes were closed as if she was asleep, but her right arm and leg were frantically, spasmodically in motion. So much so that she'd pushed off all the covers and, in the view from between the gap in the curtains around Mum's bed, the diapers around her emaciated hips and between her bony legs looked like the largest thing in the bed. They made Mum look like a caricature of a baby. Instead of pudgy little newborn legs punching the air, Mum's agitated limbs stuck out like long crooked sticks, the calf, knee, and thigh muscles that had given Mum such great-looking legs wasted away entirely. The white stocking-socks they dressed her in for warmth only emphasized how skinny she had become. From where I stood, at the gap in the curtains, she looked grotesque, repulsive. I wanted to run.

I moved to cover her, because her hospital shirt had gotten pulled up, leaving a breast exposed. But her right leg and hand wouldn't stop their frenzied movement, the leg beating a jagged circular motion as though she was pumping a bicycle uphill, her hand pushing the covers away again, reaching for her paralysed left leg, and trying to shift it. Her eyes remained closed, her mouth sagged open, a dark, toothless void. She was breathing hard, and moaning.

I took her good right hand in mine, trying to soothe her. But immediately, she snatched it away, went back to plucking at what she could grasp of the bedclothes, pulling them away again, the gaunt and wasted flesh exposed.

I can't do this, I thought. She's shut me out, she's turned away. I watched her blind, compulsive agitation. No! I had to get past it, had to find some way in, to the familiar, to Mum. She was in there, still: I had to find her. In my journal later, I wrote: "I kept diving, burrowing in." I moved right in next to Mum's head on her pillow, positioning myself close to her right ear, my left hand around her head, stroking her left temple, seeing only that: so close that the off-putting sight of her was blurred. My lips close to her ear, my voice low and steady, I kept repeating, "It's okay, it's okay," trying to tune in to us and our close connection, trying to tune out the noise, the restless leg and arm and, with it, my anxiety and the fear threatening to paralyse me and shut me down.

This was the moment, I think, that took me over the top, when grief and grieving swept me over the edge, into the flood, the ebb and flow of pure relating, pure relationship, even in the face and the dark open mouth of death. It was as though I'd learned to breathe under water.

All through the re-lived journey of mourning that writing this book has been to me, I've wrestled to understand how it changed me in the process of my having struggled to be there, intimately connected to Mum as dementia then death overtook her. As part of this, I've focused on things like the self and "the word," and our society's propensity to rank cognition and individual self-knowledge as the core of our humanity. I remember reciting, "the word made flesh" from my Sunday school catechism, not the other way around, with flesh evoking the word. Yet as a mother I learned this the other way around as I nursed and cuddled and began to play pat-a-cake with my beloved baby Donald. I learned the sequence of language acquisition, and I knew, because I was immersed in it, the deep well of love from which it pulsed, first as two bodies in one and then as two separate bodies with hands and tongues and points of view. Trying to be there with Mum in her dementia, I'd followed another learning curve, or rather an un-learning curve, that was hard, even harsh and bitter at the time, in letting go of all to which Mum's words, her cognition, and her stories had been attached. But equally I'd found myself led in another learning curve, a pulsing of breath and gestures so closely in sync that at times our two bodies became almost one again. In that moment at Mum's bedside in the geriatric wing of the Queensway Carleton Hospital, it was as though I arrived back at the beginning, to before the individual self-consciousness speaks an I and its wilful self into being. I was plunged back into the blind groping toward union and communion, the simple yearning for connection and relationship that marks us as human.

I was no longer alone. I had unlearned the lessons of self as aloof and self-sufficient, lessons of my culture, but also ones that Mum herself had taught me, perhaps out of her personal childhood feelings of abandonment after her mother's death. I think Mum had unlearned these lessons too. We'd done it together.

I think of the Latin roots of the words "spiritual" and "spirituality": *spiro, spirare, spiravi, spiratum*, which are the verb forms of the word "to breathe." It's the fundamental action connecting us to life, expressing not only the essential inter-dependence that we enact every moment of our biological existence from our first intake of breath at birth to our last exhalation at death. It's also the cultural roots of kissing, which is in sniffing and sharing one another person's breath. Historically, this includes the *conspiratsio* (meaning "breathe together"), the ritual shared kiss that, as philosopher-theologian Ivan Illich told David Cayley in the CBC Radio *Ideas* program "The Corruption of Christianity," bonded early Christians into an explicitly "spiritual community."

I think too of how important breathing is in Tibetan Buddhist practice, including the conscious giving and receiving from self to non-self that is the meditative practice of tonglen. In her lovely book *Making Friends with Death*, Buddhist teacher and pastoral counsellor Judith Lief describes tonglen as a breath-based give and take: "Breathing in what you would like to reject, breathing out what you would like to keep." On a personal level, it involves dissolving, through breathing, your resistance to things like a pain you fear, by breathing in the fear and, as you exhale, letting go of the need to conquer, to control and resist it. On a larger scale, it involves taking on others' pain and torment, including people on the verge of death, "breathing in [their] fear and breathing out to [them] your courage and companionship," Lief writes. She goes on to say that even health-care professionals report finding the tonglen approach useful in their work. She suspects this is because "it strikes at a very core point—how we barricade ourselves from pain and lose our connection with one another." Or, as religious educator David B. McCurdy puts it in an article entitled "Personhood, Spirituality, and Hope in the Care of Human Beings with Dementia" published in *The Journal of Clinical Ethics* advocating the place of spirituality especially in the institutional care of people with dementia: "spirituality encompasses—and in a strong sense *unites*—the human being who is afflicted with dementia and the human being who provides this person with care." He invokes a model of personhood similar to Martin Buber's model of I-thou reciprocity. He describes this as centred in "mutuality" and relationship and, with this, "the awareness of a deeply shared humanity—which might permit caregiver and patient to become 'means of grace' to *each other.*"

I had read nothing on this before that Sunday as I bent over Mum's head, one hand stroking her face, the other holding onto her hand for as long as she'd let me each time, calling my love into her ear, steadily repeating the same phrase "it's okay, it's okay," as I paced my voice and breath to soothe her, to calm her ragged breath. As I reached in, deeper and deeper, following my instinct, my yearning, burrowing in, it felt like the line separating my lips from her ear had somehow dissolved. It was as though I followed the sound of my own voice into Mum's ear, trying so hard to make contact that I let myself fall into a well that was all being. I don't think I was forgetting or "transcending" myself. I experienced it more as a deepening of self, into the roots of now that is also all time, into the well of life and love where the boundary between one person and another, one generation and the next, begins to blur.

I have no idea how long this went on, only that somewhere behind me, my back was shrieking with the pain of leaning so far over the bed rail. I had leaned in as close as I could initially just to get myself past the purely visual, the spectacle Mum made when viewed from outside. I kept on leaning close as I kept up my steady stream of words. I kept stroking the side of her head, holding her hand for as long as she'd tolerate this, and noticing that the intervals were getting longer. Eventually her thrashing subsided. The restlessness settled into calm. She surfaced. She never really opened her eyes, except briefly, and just a slit, to see that it was me after all, I think. Though, who knows? Perhaps to see if she was still in the land of the living. She squeezed my hand. I squeezed hers back, feeling the connection charge through me. It wasn't something tangible, more akin to pure spirit, whatever that means. Yet it was as real as the umbilical chord that had connected me to Mum in her womb.

"I love you," I said. Her lips moved, smiling slightly. Then she spoke, a mumble but clear enough: "I love you too."

A nurse or nursing aide stuck her head around the curtain. I asked if she could change Mum's diapers.

"Is that better?" I asked when she'd left.

Another half-smile in response, then, clearly: "Yes."

That evening, when I wrote of this in my journal, I finished my account of what happened then added: "It strikes me that I am being born again. Or rather, there are two things going on. I feel as though I'm serving almost as a midwife here, soothing Mum's journey toward death and acting as her trusted navigator. And in making that journey so close to her skin, so close to death, I am being born into a new sense of myself and my own aliveness: on the other side of the fear of death, on the other side of my insecurity, of my fear of living fully, my horror at the nursing-home look.

"Certainly into a new level of maturity," I continued in my journal that night. "A new stage in growing up. One not only in which I'm ready to face life without Mum, but also where death is now part of my life. Mum might not die for weeks or months yet. But this past month has taken her from living to the realm I can only describe as dying. It's been a hard month for me, each sharp decline registering like a bomb going off deep inside me, the explosion itself usually delayed until about three o'clock in the morning. But I have not looked away. I have not deflected into busyness. I have steadied myself in my focused tunnel vision. I have made friends with the sunken cheeks, the spastic hands and leg, the tossing head and closed eyes. I realize now that this is a continuum, a continuum I will follow through death until Mum takes up residence deep inside my chest where Dad turned up sometime during the year of my grieving at his death. Though this time round, I suspect that the interval of feeling lost will be shorter."

My writing that night continued: "People talk about being born again in faith. Well, if having a felt sense of life as a continuum, and minutely interconnected, if not at the level of particle, then of wave and rhythm, if that can be called faith, I think I have begun to achieve it."

Monday was a frantic teaching day: Students were beginning to research their final essays, and lined up at my door to talk about them. I was exhausted when I got home, and left a message for Doug hoping that he might go to see Mum that evening. I took the dog for a walk and went to bed early.

The next morning, I missed the call from the hospital. I was out with the dog, and didn't yet have a phone with a blinking light that would have signalled a message when I got back. They got through to Doug instead, and he assured them he'd be in as soon as he could get out of court.

It was Remembrance Day, and I normally treat the morning as sacred, a time during which I remember my great uncle Evan Bayne who was gassed in World War I, and my peaceable father wounded twice during World War II. As a peace activist, I treat it as a sort of annual recommitment as I remember war's irredeemable toll on human life and sensibilities.

By then too, I'd basically given up on the book I was writing, thinking to get Mum settled in the nursing home first. So I read the newspaper and planned to go see Mum after lunch. I picked up the phone to make a call at around 10:30, and heard the telltale beep indicating a message. I immediately phoned the hospital back.

"Your mother's not doing so well," the nurse told me. "Can you come in?"

I only had a lunch meeting to cancel then I was out the door, in my old work-at-home clothes, without a bra or even deodorant on.

They were announcing the imminent start of the two minutes of silence when I came through the front doors and, grabbing a squirt of sanitizer from the wall unit, passed through the foyer and headed for the elevators. The eleventh hour of the eleventh day of the eleventh month of the year to commemorate the exhausted end of World War 1. The reminder of the approaching hour came intermittently through the hospital intercom as I hurried down the corridor, turned left, then right into the room where they'd had Mum on Sunday. The bed was empty. The room was empty. My mouth went dry. Where was she? Where had they taken my mother?

I found a nurse just as the silence was to begin. Normally I would have fallen silent too; I always do. That day, though, I was desperate to not even let two minutes separate me from Mum. The nurse whispered the room number and pointed. I hurried back to the main corridor, turned right, and ran up the by-then still and silent stretch of linoleum until I found the room. It was a semi-private room, and only the far bed by the window was occupied, the figure hunched under covers, curled away from the door. I couldn't be sure it was Mum until I came around the foot of the bed. Yes it was. I rushed up to her head, calling "Mum," to get her to open her eyes, to bring on that radiant welcoming smile. Nothing.

I leaned my whole body over the railing, reaching for her good hand with one of mine, and cupping her head with the other. Still nothing. Her hand stayed utterly limp in mine, her eyelids emphatically closed. She was breathing hard, as though she was struggling, maybe just to wake up, but not moving a muscle.

"It's okay, Mum. It's okay, I'm here," I repeated, my face next to hers, my breath hot against her face.

No response. In the continuing silence around us, there was only the sound of Mum's harsh breathing and my own voice repeating "It's okay, Mum," then just "Ah Mum," my voice pressing the words like balm against her ear, trying to soothe her in whatever was going on for her on the other side of those flaccid eyelids. I became aware of sound resuming around us, the two minutes of silence obviously over. Still, I stayed where I was, stroking Mum's forehead, squeezing her hand, my voice low and calm, alternating between "Ah, Mum" and "It's okay" and who knows what all else. It was pure instinct speaking, pure desire to console, and make better, but not, after the first minute or so, to wake her up. Some instinct told me she couldn't.

I raised my head at the sound of someone approaching. It was one of the cleaning staff mopping the floor. She paused in her work, smiled and, nodding toward Mum, told me: "She breathing better now. She know you're here."

Oh? Oh, really? I wouldn't have known it myself. I nodded. I hope I said thanks, because it was such a gift, an affirmation, and an encouragement to keep on doing whatever gut instinct was prompting me to do. Now another person came into the room. She introduced herself as Linda Hay; she was the palliative-care nurse, she said. Immediately, everything went still inside me; it was her voice as much as anything else that alerted me: a slow and sedate contralto. It must be a job requirement.

She asked if I could step out of the room with her. I didn't want to leave Mum's side, but she quietly insisted, explaining once we were in the hall, that she didn't want Mum to overhear. She then got straight to the point. "Your mother is dying," she said. Outwardly, nothing changed. I took this in calmly. Inwardly, it was as though I'd been re-positioned against the far wall, hurled there by some unimaginable force. Linda continued in the same strong though infinitely gentle and slow-paced voice. She said that Mum was in the final stage. "It wouldn't surprise me if she were gone in twelve hours." I took this in too, felt it entering me like a soft cannonball. This was it, and I immediately deflected into performance, remaining calm and ready to do the right thing, ignoring the urgent impulse to ask: How can you be so sure?

It took me years to recover the question and some months more to track down Linda so I could ask it at last, because by this time she was retired. Although she couldn't remember the details of the case, Linda guessed that Mum had probably had another stroke. Linda had been called in when Mum had failed to wake up that morning. She'd checked the chart to see when Mum had last had something to eat or drink, since ceasing to eat and drink are markers of impending death. Then she did what she always does: she slipped a hand under the blankets to feel Mum's feet and legs. Sure enough they were cold: a sign of circulation shutting down.

As we walked back into Mum's room that November morning, Linda explained that she planned to administer a tiny dose of morphine to keep Mum's breathing calm. I asked about hydration, which Dick had mentioned once in a conversation we'd had about giving comfort. Linda advised against it, saying that it prolonged death needlessly, and wasn't necessary for the patient, and for her the patient's needs came first. I said I wanted to talk to Dick and she offered me her office to make long-distance phone calls. But she would give Mum an initial small dose of morphine now. I stood by Mum's head and spoke into her ear alerting her to what was happening. "It's going to hurt a little now," I said as Linda inserted the mosquito-sized "butterfly" needle. I stood there a bit longer, stroking Mum's forehead, telling her I loved her, gathering my strength, then I said I was going to phone the others and I'd be right back. I kissed her and slipped out of the room.

I can still remember Linda's office in vivid detail, with its low-light table lamp; its sofa with an afghan folded over one arm. The phone was on the desk. I sat down and called Dick at the Montreal Chest Institute. The secretary put me through immediately, and of course I assumed that the entire world consisted of Dick waiting to hear from me. I don't think I even started with my usual polite, "hi how are you," just blurted it right out: "Mum's dying," my voice cracking as the fact came out of my mouth. It was happening. Mum was dying, though I didn't know consciously what that meant. Dick was calm at his end of the line. He asked if I could wait a minute. There was a meeting going on in his office; he'd ask the people to leave. Meeting? I remember thinking, not being able to comprehend that there was another reality going on. Then he was back and calm. He couldn't get away, he told me. Robyn, his wife, was away and the two girls were too young to be left on their own. He asked me to keep him posted. I dragged in my breath to compose myself. Yes, I said, and moved on to practicalities. On the subject of morphine, he said, it hastens death, and advised against it. Okay, I said. I understood. Yes, I said, I'd be phoning Jan next. Doug knew already, and he'd be in soon. I dialled Jan's number in Arizona, mentally trying to calculate how early it still was there. As luck would have it the English-as-a-second-language class Jan normally taught that day had been cancelled and she was home. When I told her the news, she said she'd be on the next plane. I was surprised, and instantly afraid for her too. I gave her the hospital number and Linda's name so she could get me if I'd gone back to Mum's room, and tell me her arrival time. Then I asked if she'd like me to give Mum a message.

Oh, Jan said. Then, after a moment: "Tell her I love her and I'm on my way."

"I'll tell her," I said, my voice breaking, tears rising in my eyes, aching in my throat. I put down the phone and took a Kleenex from the box on Susan's desk. I wiped my cheeks. I blew my nose and stood up. I'd done my duty; now I could get back to Mum. I hurried down the hall.

Nothing had changed since I'd been gone, though there were some things on the night table that hadn't been there before. Linda pointed them out to me: the simple stuff of which palliative care consists. There was a jar of Vaseline, a bottle of hand lotion, a pair of thick socks, a bottle of special mouthwash and mouth swabs wrapped in crinkly clear plastic. Linda picked one up, and took off the plastic. Holding the handle in her hand, she dipped the pink sponge at the end into some mouthwash. In the same measured contralto voice, she explained that it's good to moisten the lips and freshen up the inside of the mouth. But since Mum's swallow reflex would be gone by now, it was important to get rid of any drips before inserting it into her mouth. Otherwise she might aspirate it into her lungs. I nodded, and watched Linda's careful circular motions, running the sponge along the inside of Mum's lips and on into the cavity of her toothless mouth. I followed suit, careful about the extra drop, which might be lethal. Then the intercom announced a call for Linda. It would be Jan calling back, she said, and sent me off, saying she'd still be here when I returned.

Doug and Norma had arrived when I got back. I remember seeing rubbers on Doug's shoes, and water on his coat. It must be raining, I thought. Doug was standing back and away from the bed, one arm crossed across his chest, the other raised to his face, his hand stroking his chin: His thinking posture and an effective shield. He looked at me, calm and dignified, even gentle. I touched his arm in greeting then went to Norma who handed me a bag and a Tim Horton's coffee. I have no memory of having phoned Norma from the hospital. Yet clearly I had, because the bag contained one of her bras and dedorant, and the coffee was just the way I like it. Now I put these things down and went into her arms for a hug, taking in her warm and sympathetic presence and letting my feelings come. I felt something cracking, a howl rising to the surface but immediately, conscious of Mum being able still to hear, squelched it. There were more people in the room. Someone was announcing that we'd have to pay the semi-private rate. Then someone else was being moved into the other bed. Then, just as suddenly it seemed, Linda was arranging to move Mum into the room across the hall. A single room, a private room.

Meanwhile, Doug and I had turned furiously on the officious nurse blithering on about paying. We'll pay whatever you want, just don't bother us about it now, we scathingly told her. Throughout all this time, Mum hadn't stirred. No response to my squeezing of her hand, no flicker of a smile on her lips. Only, sometimes it seemed, a sigh—of tension released, of inner fatigue, of letting go, who knows?

When the flurry of activity subsided, Mum's bed was in the room across the hall. Her memory book had been placed on the shelf by the window. Her red dressing gown was pulled up around her and the afghan from the nurse's office laid over her feet, and the slight paraphernalia that Linda had introduced me to earlier were arranged now on the nightstand beside this bed. I explained to Doug and Norma about the mouth swabs, and the importance of tapping off the drip. I had in mind that I would leave them to visit with Mum alone. I mentioned about how I had sung to Mum the other day; how it had soothed her. Norma said she was going home; she planned to make a good Scotch broth soup for everyone for supper. That left Doug and me alone with Mum. Doug was pacing. I thought now to leave him alone with Mum, and suggested I grab some lunch while he was here. I'd come back, when? In an hour? Fine, Doug said, sitting down in the visitor's chair and starting to leaf through a magazine. When I returned, Doug had moved the chair next to the bed, and had one hand under the covers, holding Mum's hand.

When he left, the room was utterly quiet, except for the sound of Mum's steady, light breathing, and mine alongside it keeping pace. I stroked Mum's hair back from her forehead. Her skin felt cool. I pulled the red dressing gown higher. Then I took the socks, and lifted the bed covers. Her feet were waxy-white and cold. I took one foot in my warm and still vital hands, remembering Mum in high heels, or those cheap bargain-basement sneakers she wore when walking the length of the barn roof tarring the nail holes on hot July days. I stroked the still-baby-soft skin at the base of her toes, then gently pulled the warm sock over them, eased the wool up over her arch, around her calloused heel and up around her scrawny ankle. I did this knowing the gesture was pointless, though not for me. I was marking and making my way into the next phase of mourning, of letting go and letting in what life brings moment by successive moment. It was as though I was bathing Mum's feet; without fully realizing it, I was preparing the body. All its heat was being extinguished. I was bearing witness, paying homage.

I'd been a remote bystander at my father's death. This time round, I was more even than an attentive observer. I had become an insider, inside the experience, making it my own, letting it change me utterly as it brought me here into this room, within the circumference of Mum's dying breath. To the extent that I got here, came to understand death and let it into my life, I did it through these small gestures and actions, although I have only come to understand this after the fact. At the time, I was going entirely on instinct and intuition: both what I wanted to do to be there with Mum, and what I needed to do to be there for myself. Putting the socks on Mum's feet became a ritual, a medium for taking in what was happening, and understanding it at a level well below thought and rational consciousness. In covering Mum's feet with the socks, removing them from my sight for all time, I was participating in their removal from this earth. That part of Mum's existence, that way of her being in the world was gone, just as those shoes bagged up in the clear plastic hospital bag a month ago when she'd fallen and broken her hip had in fact been redundant, no longer part of her life. Some part of me understood this now and, past resisting it, helped smooth the way.

The job done, I tenderly covered her legs back up, tucked the bedclothes close in around her body and smoothed them nicely, aware as I did so that she'd never be pulling them off again. The time of her agitation, of action of any kind in this world, was over. I went back to the head of the bed. I glanced at the stuff on the nightstand, as though looking for inspiration. The hand lotion. Mum's right hand was tucked in like a child's under her chin on the bed. I gently pulled it forward and then, with a dollop of lotion on my fingers, began massaging her hand. As my fingers caressed all the wrinkles and age spots of her skin, I found myself talking to Mum, as though we were having a conversation, telling her all the things I was going to remember. Sometimes I began "Remember—?" as though we were reminiscing together. Linda had told me that it was important to let the dying person know it was okay for them to go, to give them permission. Yet I hesitated, thinking of Jan on a plane somewhere, trying to make it go faster, to get her here in time. I'd already asked that no further morphine be given, and Linda had complied, though reminding me that the patient has to come first at this point. So I told Mum she'd done a fine job in this life. I also told her that I loved her and she would always be with me. As I wrote in my journal afterward, "I felt totally uninhibited as the afternoon breathed along, in and out." I had nothing to get off my chest, no distance to navigate between us. I had nothing to do but stay tuned to this breathing, sometimes slightly sighing and unmoving woman beside me, inwardly dreaming her way to some place, some time utterly beyond my reach.

I told Mum I was going to rinse out her mouth again then opened another of the plastic wrappers, soaked the pink plastic foam with the mouthwash then tapped it on the side so that there was no risk of loose liquid running down Mum's throat and her helpless to stop it. I ran the sponge along the inside of her upper and lower lips, then on either side of her tongue. At one point, I thought she tried to clamp hold of the sponge, to suck, to hold as though to squeeze my hand, who knows? But mostly, there was nothing, no response to my gesture. No movement whatsoever. And that was okay. I felt totally calm, at peace, adrift in this lovely long moment of time we had alone together.

After washing out Mum's mouth, I pulled the chair in close, plunked a pillow down on its arm, perched myself upon it, leaned in across the railing until my breath at least was touching Mum's face, and I started to sing. I sang all the songs I'd sung to her less than a week ago, when she'd still been awake and alert enough to smile, to squeeze my hand and say "lovely, lovely."

Now she was too removed from her lips and hands to respond. Yet I could hear the echo of her voice from last week, and I carried on, knowing that hearing and the capacity to feel emotions are the last to go.

It didn't matter if my voice broke now. There was nobody else around, and it was too much work and bother trying to hold myself tightly together at this point. I remembered a poem I had memorized one day as a child, all in one sitting, when I'd arrived home from school in time to catch Mum still upstairs on her bed with her tea and her latest Perry Mason murder-mystery. The poem was "When Day is Done" by Henry Longfellow. If I could remember it all now, I would recite it for Mum one last time.

Leaning as close as I could to Mum's body in the hospital bed, my forehead fused to hers, I began: "When day is done, and the darkness falls from the wings of Night as a feather is wafted downward from an eagle in its flight. I see the lights of the village gleam through the rain and the mist, and a feeling of sadness comes o'er me that my soul cannot resist. . . ." My voice broke down completely, but I carried on to the very end that describes how, at the sound of a familiar voice reciting simple lines of familiar poetry, all the cares of the day "shall fold their tents like the Arabs, and as silently steal away." Silence as I wept, "stealing away" throbbing in my chest. Then I told Mum I was coming to have a snooze with her and, very matter-of-factly as though it was the most natural thing in the world and something I did all the time, I climbed over the railing of the bed. Carefully, I slid my body into the space next to Mum's, my back pressed hard against the rails. My body cupped Mum's age-shrunken back, my chin settled onto a bony shoulder. I think I murmured something like "Good night, sleep tight," then I settled into the rhythm of her breathing, my breath answering hers, the exhalation quiet against the wrinkled skin on the back of her neck, my nostrils taking in the slightly sour smell of her unwashed hair. I think I drifted off to sleep because something—the door opening—startled me, and I opened my eyes. But it was just a nurse checking in, and she quickly and quietly withdrew. I lay there a while longer, taking in Mum's smell, the feel of her knobby shoulder bone digging into the soft flesh under my chin. Then I peeled myself carefully away from where I'd been lying, feeling the chill of the air where I'd grown warm from pressing against Mum's body, taking that in too, the sharp knowing pain of it. I clambered carefully over the railing, and placed my feet back down on the floor.

Still the quiet contained us, time flowing in and out with our breath. I had to pee, badly, so I forced myself to walk the three steps away from Mum's bed into the ensuite bathroom just beyond it. When I returned, I leaned over the railing and spoke into Mum's ear, saying I was going to wash out her mouth again then maybe go and get us some tea. By now, I had the routine down pat. My hand had learned the contours of Mum's mouth. I slid the sponge along her upper gum line, then under her tongue and around the lower gums. There wasn't the slightest movement of muscle. I didn't think of it as shutting down, more as Mum no longer needing muscles and legs and voice and a throat for swallowing, not where she was going. I felt she was in a body of water, flowing water, a river or a canal. I thought of it as a sort of birth canal, as though Mum was being delivered out of this world in a reverse version of how she'd entered it eighty-five years ago. I also felt that she'd been lost and floundering earlier, when I arrived in the morning. It was as though she'd been banging on the roof of her eyelids, trying to wake up the normal way. But now she'd got herself turned around, like a baby turning in the womb as it prepares to enter the world. It was dark where she was, and yet I felt she knew where she was going. She had her bearings. She wasn't afraid. I was sure of that, although I also had a sense that my voice steadily talking or singing in her ear was somehow helping. Maybe she could feel my hand holding hers too, stroking the skin of her face, and that was helping too. Certainly it was keeping us connected, and that helped me.

I told the nurse that I wanted to get some tea, and immediately a palliative-care volunteer appeared to sit with Mum while I was gone. I felt instantly relieved about going, though hurried so as not to be away long. When I returned, the volunteer had the memory book open in her lap, and expressed great interest in the life Mum had led. Yes, I said, and we both looked at Mum, a small, shrunken figure in the bed. A number of nurses had commented on the memory book over the last week or so that it had been on Mum's nightstand. They'd obviously flipped through it when they had a quiet moment, and I like to think it helped them to see Mum as a person, not just a body needing total care in every functional category.

The woman stood up to leave. "Is there anything you need?" she asked.

"I need a hug," I recorded in my journal as having replied.

"Oh," she said, her face and arms opening simultaneously. As soon as she touched me, I broke into tears. I sobbed; though, aware of Mum, not wanting to upset her, I quickly stopped.

"Thank you," I said.

"That's what we're here for," she said, smiling, and left.

Two nurses came in both to turn Mum and to "refresh" her, the euphemism for changing her diaper. They expected me to leave, but made no comment when I said that I would stay. I watched them as they undid the tabs, pulled the bulky front part of it away and observed that she was dry. This meant that her kidneys had shut down, the male nurse observed. I took that in, and continued watching as they powdered her skin and readjusted the tabs. Then he took a hot washcloth and gently washed Mum's face. I wanted to be doing that; wished that I could take over from him, but kept quiet. He was doing it with such dignity. When they left, I resumed my post beside Mum's head, the better for her to hear any little thing I might say. I opened the jar, and put some Vaseline on Mum's lips. Then I got out my hairbrush, and brushed Mum's hair back from the pillow. I was finishing this when Doug walked in. It was nearly five already: He'd come straight from the office. I offered him the last of my tea, told him that nothing much had changed, and cleared my stuff off the chair so he could sit down. I didn't want to leave. My whole being was centred here, in Mum's breathing and the bits of care and comfort I could give her. Still, I wanted to give Doug more time alone with Mum. We agreed that he'd sit with her while I went home to feed the dog and take a break. Then, sure, I said, I'd go pick up Norma on the way back to the hospital. When? In an hour or so? That's fine, Doug said, and set down his things.

I bent toward Mum and kissed her. I told her I'd be back soon then I left.

Night had fallen, and the rain had turned into a mist that felt like silk against my face. Back home, I got on the phone to Donald. "Your granny's dying," I said, my voice breaking. "I need a hug." I also told him that I wanted to go for a walk, and wanted him to come with me by the river, for safety and company. He walked the few blocks over, and awkwardly wrapped his arms around me.

"I'm sorry. I'm drunk," he said as he stepped away.

"That's okay, you're here," I replied. Then, with the dog and

poop bag in hand, we set off toward the banks of the Ottawa River. Moisture hung in the still air, muffling everything, uniting everything. I spoke a little about the day, what the palliative-care nurse had said, the fact that Janet was on her way, that we'd be meeting her plane at eleven. I sighed.

"You're sad," he said.

"Yes," I said.

"Me too," he replied. I looked up at him, this lovely child of mine still struggling to accept his chronic illness. I smiled and slipped my arm through his, my hand seeking his hand, my fingers lacing with his, and squeezed.

Donald was ready to turn around and go back. It was probably well past six by then; time to head back to the hospital. By then we had walked into a little bay, where the water lies still and quiet on a ledge of layered limestone. I asked Donald to wait, and walked to the water's edge. I sank down on my heels, and scooped up some water to wash my face. Then I stayed where I was, hunched down, and looked out over the water, where it rippled up into the current just beyond this inner bay. I was aware of Donald coming up and, soundlessly, squatting down beside me. I continued to stare out over the water. And as I looked, a thought came to me, clear and whole and totally out of the blue: She's entered the river of souls.

Tears came to my eyes. I blinked and looked out over the water, amazed because it was as though the words had been spoken directly into my mind.

I said the words out loud to Donald, just as they'd come to me. He nodded; this made perfect sense to him. We stood up. We turned back. Time to go pick up Norma.

Epilogue

Some weeks or months later, I asked Doug if some day he would tell me about the last minutes of Mum's life, since I had been away from her bed from around five until she died at around 6:30. Many months later, he mailed me, Dick, and Jan his account, which he'd titled, "Now I Lay Me Down to Sleep." I unfolded the pages and read.

I had been, truth to tell, catching up on some homework. I had a file open in the deep window well of her dying room (a private space in the busy hospital to accommodate the sensibilities of the acutely ill and the palpable evidence of human frailty or medicine's inevitable failure). I was pacing a narrow space between her single bed and the generous window on which, one by one, I would spread out the file on which I was working or the pile of correspondence I was getting through. Mother needed little from me or the nursing staff. There would be moments when she would grimace, and occasionally her breath would catch. All that was needed was a hand to hold her hand, or to smooth a cloth over her forehead, although there wasn't a fevered forehead to cool. In fact, she seemed to be getting cooler to the touch.

The warm cloth seemed to provide comfort. She turned her face yearningly, with her unopened eyes, following the caress of the cloth, and then she subsided, the effort exhausting her store of energy for that half hour. The coma reclaimed her.

I stopped reading, amazed. Mum had moved? She had turned her face "yearningly" in response to this gesture from her first-born son? Was this possible? I asked Linda Hay, the palliative-care nurse who had been with Mum that day. Oh yes, she said. At some level, Mum might have understood that Doug was there. This was her way of saying "I love you" one last time. And also, I thought, acknowledging his love for her, at last.

Doug's account continued:

Twice in the last hour my mother made a noise. In both cases it was quiet—more an interruption in the regular and quiet susurration of her breath, like a person suffering from sleep apnea. In both cases, as I came to her bed, the spasm passed. In one case, she was frowning, but with a hand on her forehead, she smiled reflexively. The second time there was only a slight increase in breathing, like an imitation of panting, and then she slowed and settled

I finished one tape and was in the process of changing to another when some tiny noise turned me back to the bed. I thought there was a catch in her breath, and I came over to take her hand. The breathing didn't pick back up. There was one entire moment of perfect silence while I held my own breath and bent over, and then the crushing realization that she was dying or dead panicked me. I put her hand down and jostled her shoulder. I pushed her shoulder back so as to have her lie flat on her back so I could push on her chest. As I did that, I realized the incredible fragility of her. Her shoulder was a skeleton clothed in dry skin, and I realized I could no more press down on her chest without crushing her, as if I knew what I was doing anyway. I fumbled for the button and couldn't find it. I raced out of the room to the nurses' station. A nurse, seeing my stricken face, came instantly. She turned on the main light as she came into the room, and the room went from being a part of the night outside to being a part of the hospital, and my mother was a thin and careless corpse lying dishevelled, half uncoiled from her fetal position, one arm sprawled out beside her. The nurse moved quickly but unhurriedly to her, taking up her hand and feeling for the pulse at the wrist and with her other hand, feeling for the pulse under the jaw line. As she did so, her head turned to me and she made one small gesture, shaking her head sideways—once, twice.

"NO."

I wanted to do something, for her to do something, for her to call in those teams of people you see on television with rushing stretchers and electric pads in both hands, shouting "clear, clear." Instead, all was quiet—silent. I asked, in a whisper (who would hear?) whether we should do anything, whether I could do anything. The nurse again shook her head, no. She was counting, I think, under her breath. After a minute, she put my mother's hand down and said simply, "She's dead."

All the world gets smaller when your mother dies. No phalanx of forebears now stand between us and our own dates with old age, disease, and death. Most of all, overwhelmingly, I felt grief as a blow buckling the knees and making the room spin. But there were the mundane, even comedic details to help get past the moment. The nurse asked me what position I wanted her in. It took me a moment to realize because rigor mortis was going to set in and we had to arrange her in a position. In the end, the nurse and I helped straighten her out, lying on her back, with her hands crossed over each other at the wrist, over her chest like a crusader from a gravestone rubbing. Next, the nurse asked me whether I wanted to have my mother's teeth in. How do you decide such things?

"In," I said. She and I tried our best to get the full set of dentures back inside my mother's mouth. In the end I stopped trying to assist because my diffidence in touching my mother's lips and mouth meant I was not helping but simply getting in the way. The nurse finished the job but they looked awful. The lips wouldn't close over them and they looked hideously artificial and out of place.

"Out," I said. That was worse. The mouth now gaped open.

"In," I said.

And then she left, to bring in a doctor who had to certify the death, the time, and the cause. Old age, I felt like saying—a tumult of insult, a litany of diseases, and medical misfortunes, a dirge of an empty and lonely life . . . I had my cellphone and a list of people I had to call, but I had this quiet moment to come forward, to bend down over her and to cup her face, still warm, with my hands, and to kiss her on the cheeks, on the forehead and on the lips.

"Good night, Mother."

When Norma and I arrived half an hour later, the bars on the bed were down; no danger of Mum falling out of bed now.

Seeing them down, Mum so obviously beyond the need of their protection anymore, I burst into tears, flung myself against her body, and howled. But not for long. In fact, I felt amazingly calm, serene almost. I joined Doug with Norma at the foot of the bed. We spoke in soft voices about what was to be done next. Mum had decided years ago to donate her body to medical science, and there was a document about this to give to the appropriate authorities. Plus, Jan's plane wasn't due till eleven. I wanted them to leave Mum's body exactly as it was so we could bring Jan in to see, to take in fully, when she got here. Norma said she would have the soup ready for us when we were finished, took Doug's car and left Doug and me to these matters.

Norma's Scotch broth was amazing. I couldn't get over how delicious it was, the flavours rising up through my tongue, the aroma through my nose. Of course, I hadn't really eaten all day. But I had an appetite I've rarely experienced before, as though my senses had been released back to me, and were exulting in being alive. I was hugely, unabashedly hungry. I had a second bowlful and even sucked on the bone.

Then Doug and I were at the airport, and Jan was on the escalator descending into the arrivals area, an expectant look and a smile on her face. As she walked away from the base of the staircase, we walked toward her and, without a word, folded her into our arms. We stood there, our three sets of arms around each other, breathing, and I hoped that Jan would get the message from our bodies.

She pulled away. "So," she said, looking at our faces with that same expectant look.

"She's gone," I said. Doug said something about "too late," and again, we folded Jan into our arms and stood there holding each other tight.

Dick arrived the next day after he'd got the girls up and off to school. By then they'd removed Mum's body from the hospital to the funeral home for which Jan had arranged months earlier. She would stay there until the closest medical school arranged a transfer. It was hard complying with this thing Mum had always spoken of doing: Giving her body to the science she had nearly gone into herself, a final gesture of love and respect perhaps for her father and his chosen life's work of medicine. Yet for those remaining, and grieving, it meant having to postpone any cremation or burial; whatever teaching hospital receives the body reserves the right to keep it for as long as they can make use of it for medical students learning anatomy and the diseases that ravage the body.

Still, we managed some send-off. With minimal discussion, we improvised what became a last cup of tea with Mum in one of the visitation rooms at the funeral home. We chose our own flowers to bring with us. We picked up her tea things from her room in the residence. We arrived at the funeral home with all this stuff then asked that they fill up the kettle. I remember an initial frown and raised eyebrow, but that's all; someone took the kettle and brought it back full, and we plugged it into a wall socket in the room.

Mum wasn't in a coffin. Jan had refused the funeral home's best efforts to supply one, not seeing the point of the expense, and knowing Mum wouldn't either. In fact, when Jan had broached the subject of death and a funeral with Mum that autumn back in 2000 when I brought her to Arizona while I arranged her move to a residence, Mum had been clear and matter of fact. She wanted nothing, no fuss or bother. "Just scatter my ashes to the winds," she said. "Just remember me as someone who smiled and argued a lot."

The funeral home had laid her out on a sort of gurney bed, very plain, with a blanket pulled up to her neck, possibly the velour dressing gown on top; I can't remember. Whatever the details, she looked relatively unchanged from the way she'd looked last in the hospital. Except she was utterly, utterly still.

We spoke in hushed tones as we made the tea. Then we poured milk and tea into Mum's favourite cup, the lovely one she drank from every time she and I had had tea in the residence. We moved a plant pedestal close to the head of her bed, and placed the full teacup on it, as though within easy reach of her hand. Then we took up our own cups and sat around close by. We drank our tea and talked, saying things about Mum, sometimes directly to her as if she was still actively with us.

The tea was gone, the cups gathered up. An awkward silence settled in. The end? I suggested we sing one of the songs Jan had learned in Girl Guide camp, and had taught us all in the long weekend drives to and from the farm. "Kumbaya," meaning, "Come by here." Its verses touch on various stations in the journey of life, the moments of laughing and joy, the moments of sorrow and death.

As we sang the last verse, "Someone's dying, Lord, Kumbaya," the same line repeated three times, we the Menzies children broke down and cried. Not a lot. But enough to release us, to let us release Mum to wherever she was going now.

Acknowledgements

My first thanks goes to Linda McKnight, mentor and informal literary agent, who helped me shape my ideas into a book proposal; Linda Pruessen at Key Porter who believed in it; Carol Harrison, my editor whose keen intelligence helped shape the manuscript and clarify its prose, and whose generous heart helped me through a difficult patch. I also want to thank various people who gave generously of their time and knowledge: Marg Eisner, Linda Hay, Inge Loy-English, Linda Garcia, J.B. Orange, Gail Fawcett, Callista Kelly and her colleagues in Interlibrary Loans at Carleton University, Sandy Duncan, Maureen Kellerman, Pat Mayberry, and Angela Sumegi and, for crucial data retrievel, the people at Eternal Flow Computers on Gabriola and Paulo and Tianko at PC Cyber Computers in Ottawa. I am also deeply grateful to my siblings, Doug, Jan, and Dick, for their love and trust in letting me bring their private words and actions into the public domain. Finally, I want to gratefully acknowledge the financial support of the Canada Council of the Arts, the Ontario Arts Council, and the City of Ottawa. Subsistence grants from these taxpayer-supported cultural bodies gave me the time I needed to write this book.

Recommended Reading

Anonymous. *The Cloud of Unknowing*. Mahwah, NJ: Paulist Press, 1981

Pauline Boss. *Ambiguous Loss: Learning to Live with Unresolved Grief.* Cambridge, MA: Harvard University Press, 2000.

Anne Brener. *Mourning and Mitzvah: A Guided Journal for Walking the Mourner's Path through Grief to Healing*. Woodstock, VT: Jewish Lights Pub, 2001.

Allen Buchanan and Dan W. Brock. *Deciding for Others: The Ethics of Surrogate Decision Making*. Cambridge: Cambridge University Press, 1990.

Maggie Callanan and Patricia Kelley. *Final Gifts: Understanding the Special Awareness, Needs and Communications of the Dying*. New York: Walker & Co., 1995.

Ruth Campbell and Martin Conway. *Broken Memories: Case Studies in Memory Impairment*. Oxford: Blackwell Publishers, 1995.

Dr. David Kuhl. *What Dying People Want: Practical Wisdom for the End of Life*. New York: PublicAffairs, 2003.

Judith Lief. *Making Friends with Death*. New York: PublicAffairs, 2002.

Vrenia Ivonoffski, Dr. Gail Mitchell, and Dr. Christine Jones-Smith. *I'm Still Here*, DVD. Waterloo, ON: Murray Alzheimer Research and Education Program, 2006.

Judith McCann-Beranger. *A Caregiver's Guide for Alzheimer's Disease and other Dementias*. Toronto: Alzheimer Society, 2000.

Beth Witrogen McLeod. *Caregiving: The Spiritual Journey of Love, Loss, and Renewal*. Toronto: John Wiley& Sons, 1999.

Joanne Parrent. *Courage to Care: A Caregiver's Guide Through Each Stage of Alzheimer's*. New York: Alpha Books, 2001.

Sogyal Rinpoche. *The Tibetan Book of Living and Dying*. San Francisco: HarperSanFrancisco, 1994.

Joyce Rupp. *Praying our Goodbyes*. Notre Dame, IN: Ave Maria Press, 1988.

Steven R. Sabat. *The Experience of Alzheimer's Disease: LifeThrough a Tangled Veil*. Oxford: Blackwell Publishing, 2001.

Dr. Oliver Sacks. *The Man Who Mistook His Wife for a Hat*. New York: Perennial Library, 1987.

———. *Musicophilia*. New York: Knopf, 2007.

Daniel L. Schacter. *Searching for Memory: The Brain, the Mind, and the Past*. New York: Basic Books, 1996.

Jean Vanier. *Becoming Human*. Toronto: House of Anansi Press, 1998.